Post Truth

Post Truth

THE NEW WAR ON TRUTH
AND HOW TO FIGHT BACK

MATTHEW D'ANCONA

EBURY
PRESS

9 10

Ebury Press, an imprint of Ebury Publishing
20 Vauxhall Bridge Road
London SW1V 2SA

Ebury Press is part of the Penguin Random House group of companies
whose addresses can be found at global.penguinrandomhouse.com

Penguin
Random House
UK

First published by Ebury Press in 2017

www.penguin.co.uk

A CIP catalogue record for this book is available from the British Library

ISBN 9781785036873

Printed and bound in Great Britain by Clays Ltd, St Ives PLC

MIX
Paper from
responsible sources
FSC® C018179

Penguin Random House is committed to a sustainable future
for our business, our readers and our planet. This book is made
from Forest Stewardship Council® certified paper.

In memory of my mother

Helen d'Ancona (1937–2014)

A life-long truth-teller

CONTENTS

PREFACE: NEAR-DEATH, POST-TRUTH

In September 2016 I had a brush with the Grim Reaper. Suffice it to say that a perforated ulcer compounded by abdominal sepsis is not good news; or, to put it another way, I am glad that I didn't see the fatality rates until I was out of hospital.

I felt extraordinarily fortunate, though guilty about the worry I had caused my family. I also felt profound gratitude to the doctors who had saved me and helped me recover more quickly than first anticipated. I marvelled at the medical science that had brought me back from the brink: because the brink is a place where 'experts' – so often reviled these days – are just what you need.

To adapt Dr Johnson, such experiences do concentrate the mind. Once discharged, I had a single professional objective: to be back on the journalistic beat for the US presidential election on 8 November.[1] Though, like most political commentators, I expected Hillary

Clinton to win, I was convinced that Donald Trump's capture of the Republican nomination was more than an anomaly – a wrinkle in the political fabric that would soon be smoothed over. His victory made it ludicrous to argue that this was business as usual (though some tried). I was struck that my teenage sons, neither of them Trump supporters, were not remotely surprised by the outcome. Their generation had intuited a change in the air of which mine had been mostly oblivious.

But what change? Inescapably, Trump stalks the pages of this book like an orange panther. But he is not its prime subject. Nor is this a book about the far Right, or any particular ideology. It is quite straightforward to imagine a Left-wing counterpart to Trump surging to power on a wave of falsehood and phony populism. The problem lies deeper.

My theme is epistemological – which is to say, related to knowledge, its nature and its transmission. Specifically, I explore the declining value of truth as society's reserve currency, and the infectious spread of pernicious relativism disguised as legitimate scepticism. If indeed we live in a Post-Truth era, where do its roots lie? What are its principal symptoms? And what can we do about it?

Generally speaking I share Saul Bellow's distaste for 'crisis chatter'. That said, there are times when it is wrong to stay silent and affect the pose of the professionally unruffled. After more than twenty-five years as a journalist I would be betraying my trade if I stood by as its central value – accuracy – was degraded by hucksters and snake-oil salesmen. Those of us who work for the print media get things wrong, but we are also held to account for our mistakes: rightly so. So what happens when lies not only proliferate but also seem to matter less – or even not at all?

I am also a trustee of the Science Museum in London. In its stunning halls and galleries, the work of its remarkable team, it feels like an affront to the greatest revolution in the history of human knowledge that so much fakery, pseudo-science and medical nonsense is now in circulation. The notion of science as a conspiracy rather than a world-changing field of inquiry used to be confined to cranks. No longer. It seems to me intolerable that this should be so.

I mention these details because this short book is essentially a personal tract, rather than a dispassionate primer. This is not a moment for hysteria. Equally, it is no time to be sanguine, or loftily confident that what we call Post-Truth is merely the latest fashion on the intellectual catwalk and one that will fade into insignificance of its own accord.

As so often, George Orwell provides a text for our times as well as for his own – in this case, in his 1942 essay 'Looking Back on the Spanish War'. He recalled the terrifying success of Fascist propaganda, especially concerning Russian intervention in the conflict:

This kind of thing is frightening to me, because it often gives me the feeling that the very concept of objective truth is fading out of the world. After all, the chances are that those lies, or at any rate similar lies, will pass into history. How will the history of the Spanish war be written? If Franco remains in power his nominees will write the history books, and (to stick to my chosen point) that Russian army which never existed will become historical fact, and schoolchildren will learn about it generations hence. But suppose Fascism is finally defeated and some kind of democratic government restored in Spain in the fairly near future; even then how is the history of the war to be written? What kind of records will Franco have left behind him? Suppose even that the records kept on the Government side are recoverable – even so, how is a true history of the war to be written? For, as I have pointed out already, the Government also dealt extensively in lies. From the anti-Fascist angle one could write a broadly truthful history of the war, but it would be a partisan history, unreliable on every minor point. Yet, after all, *some* kind of history will be written, and after those who actually remember the war are dead. It will be universally accepted. So for all practical purposes the lie will have become truth.

There was, Orwell fully acknowledged, nothing new in the notion of historical bias. But 'what is peculiar to our own age is the abandonment of the idea that history *could* be truthfully written'.[2]

This was an early premonition of the Post-Truth era. Orwell feared that totalitarianism would be the force that destroyed the very notion of veracity. As we shall see, the pressures bearing down upon truth today are more complex, dispersed and insidious. But they are also more unsettling precisely because they do not emanate from an identifiable Big Brother or Goebbels or *Izvestia*. There is no single statue to bring crashing to the ground.

This is another reason why it is so important to see Trump as consequence rather than cause. His departure from political office – whenever that day comes – will not mark the end of the Post-Truth era, and it is a grave error of analysis to think otherwise. This is not a battle between liberals and conservatives. It is a battle between two ways of perceiving the world, two fundamentally different approaches to reality: and as between those two, you *do* have to choose. Are you content for the central value of the Enlightenment, of free societies and of democratic discourse, to be trashed by charlatans – or not? Are you on the pitch, or content to stay on the terraces?

For all the talk of public apathy and disengagement – some of it justified, some not – I remain an optimist. I think, in spite of the psychological tricks that we play on ourselves, we are ultimately hardwired to demand veracity and to resist falsehood. There is a voice within each of us that resists lies, even if that voice has (for reasons we shall see) been muted. The challenge is to turn that voice from a whisper to a roar. The truth is out there – if only we demand it.

Matthew d'Ancona
March 2017

1

'WHO CARES?': THE COMING OF THE POST-TRUTH ERA

BREXIT, TRUMP AND THE NEW POLITICAL AUDIENCE

To every thing there is a season: 1968 marked the revolution in personal freedom and the yearning for social progress; 1989 will be remembered for the collapse of totalitarianism; and 2016 was the year that definitively launched the era of 'Post-Truth'. It is the nature, origins and challenges of that era that this book seeks to address.

We have entered a new phase of political and intellectual combat, in which democratic orthodoxies and institutions are being shaken to their foundations by a wave of ugly populism. Rationality is threatened by emotion, diversity by nativism, liberty by a drift towards autocracy. More than ever, the practice of politics is perceived as a zero-sum game, rather than a contest between ideas. Science is treated with suspicion and, sometimes, open contempt.

At the heart of this global trend is a crash in the value of truth, comparable to the collapse of a currency or a stock. Honesty and accuracy are no longer assigned the highest priority in political exchange. As candidate and President, Donald Trump has demeaned the assumption that the leader of the free world should have at least a glancing acquaintance with the truth: according to the Pulitzer Prize-winning fact-checking site Politi-Fact, 69 per cent of his statements are 'Mostly False', 'False' or 'Pants on Fire'.[1] In the United Kingdom, the campaign to leave the European Union triumphed with slogans that were demonstrably untrue or misleading – but also demonstrably resonant.

Conspiracist websites and social media scorn the 'dead tree press' or MSM (mainstream media) as the discredited voice of a 'globalist' order, a 'liberal elite' whose time is past. 'Experts' are vilified as an ill-intentioned cartel rather than a source of verifiable information. 'Dare to know' was Immanuel Kant's proposed motto for the Enlightenment. Today's counterpart is: 'Dare not to'.

It is no accident that Oxford Dictionaries selected 'Post-Truth' as its word of the year in 2016, defining it as shorthand for 'circumstances in which objective facts are less influential in shaping public opinion than appeals to emotion and personal belief'.[2] Its precise etymology is disputed, though there is general consensus that it was first deployed in a 1992 article in the *Nation* by the Serbian-American writer Steve Tesich. So traumatised were the American people by Watergate, Iran–Contra and other scandals (Tesich declared) that they had started to turn away from truth, and collude wearily in its suppression:

> We are rapidly becoming prototypes of a people that totalitarian monsters could only drool about in their dreams. All the dictators up to now have had to work hard at suppressing the truth. We, by our actions, are saying that this is no longer necessary, that we have acquired a spiritual mechanism that can denude truth of any significance. In a very fundamental way we, as a free people, have freely decided that we want to live in some post-truth world.[3]

In 2010, the blogger David Roberts surveyed the latest findings of academic political science to reach similar conclusions, albeit from a different perspective. Comforting as it was to imagine that voters gathered facts, drew conclusions from those facts, formed 'issue positions' based on their conclusions and chose a political party accordingly, electoral behaviour did not conform to this ideal. In practice, Roberts wrote, they chose a party on the basis of value affiliations, adopted the opinions of the tribe, developed arguments to support those opinions and (only then) selected facts to reinforce those contentions: 'We live in post-truth politics: a political culture in which politics (public opinion and media narratives) have become almost entirely disconnected from policy (the substance of legislation). This obviously dims any hope of reasoned legislative compromise.'[4]

In 2016, the prophecies of Tesich and Roberts were realised, to spectacular effect. The election of Trump as America's forty-fifth President and the triumphant campaign to lead Britain out of the EU undoubtedly marked an uprising against the established order and a demand for ill-defined change: respectively, to 'Make America Great Again' and to 'Take Back Control'. Both victories overturned the blithe predictions of pundits, pollsters and bookies. Both blasted light across a transformed landscape whose emergence the political and media class had failed to register. Most conspicuously, both insurgencies reflected a new and alarming collapse in the power of truth as an engine of electoral conduct. Roberts's blogged thesis had become geopolitical reality.

Donald J. Trump is lionised by his supporters as a businessman uncontaminated by politics. He is hailed as the master of the deal, the balance sheet and value for money. But – as the first Post-Truth President – he is much better understood as an entertainer than as a politician or as a tycoon (who has, after all, filed for bankruptcy six times).[3] It is no accident that he tweeted so angrily when mocked by *Saturday Night Live*, or attacked by Meryl Streep at the Golden Globes. When Arnold Schwarzenegger took over his former starring role as host of *The Celebrity Apprentice*, he used Twitter to deliver his verdict: 'Wow, the ratings are in and Arnold Schwarzenegger got "swamped" (or destroyed) by comparison to the ratings machine, DJT.' Even as his transition faltered, the President-elect was not too busy for a photo-op with Kanye West.

Amazingly, Trump is a member of the World Wrestling Entertainment Hall of Fame, having engaged in a supposedly impromptu fight with Vince McMahon, the chairman of the $1.5 billion global wrestling franchise, at 'WrestleMania' in 2007. The French philosopher Roland Barthes famously categorised wrestling as 'a sum of spectacles'. Could there be a better way of describing the behaviour of this President?

'There is no more problem of truth in wrestling than in theatre,' wrote Barthes, a formulation that sounds ominously familiar in the era of 'Post-Truth'. The performance is 'episodic but always opportune', presenting an 'amorphous baseness' and 'the ever-entertaining image of the grumbler, endlessly confabulating about his displeasure'. The spectator revels in 'the emotional

magniloquence, the repeated paroxysms, the exasperation of the retorts'.[6]

None of this is a distraction for Trump: it is essential
both to his identity and his perception of the public
as an audience consuming entertainment rather than
a civically engaged electorate. His priorities are not
policy, personnel or diplomacy. Instead, he has recast
the presidency as the most desirable role in show business, part of a continuum that has stretched, for him,
from the WWE ring via film cameos to the Oval Office.
Streep and the cast of *SNL* are not just his enemies, but
fellow performers – peers and rivals. In such a context,
it must seem laughably old-fashioned to approach
government as the forging of evidence-based policy and
the pursuit of political support needed to implement it.
What counts is ratings.

This is why the President was so exercised by reports
that his inauguration had been more sparsely attended
than Barack Obama's in 2009. On the morning after
the ceremony, Trump spoke personally to the acting
director of the National Park Service, Michael T.
Reynolds, demanding additional images that would
undermine this proliferating story. On the same day,
Sean Spicer, the new White House press secretary,
called a special press conference and insisted belliger-
ently that 'this was the largest audience to ever witness
an inauguration, period, both in-person and around
the globe'. The crowd in the 2009 photographs looked

larger, he claimed, because of new white floor coverings laid on the National Mall which had the effect of 'highlighting areas where people were not standing, while in years past, the grass eliminated this visual'. The Trump administration, he warned, intended to 'hold the press accountable'.[7]

As angry as Spicer and his boss might be, their position was hilariously unsustainable. It fell to Kellyanne Conway, senior aide to the President, to find some way of squaring the epistemological circle, of reconciling bogus claim with photographic evidence. On NBC's *Meet the Press* the next day, Conway told Chuck Todd that there was a perfectly reasonable explanation: 'Don't be so overly dramatic about it, Chuck. You're saying it's a falsehood [...] Sean Spicer, our press secretary, gave alternative facts to that.'[8]

As it happens, this was not the first time a Trump supporter had advanced an argument of this sort. In December 2016, the conservative commentator Scottie Nell Hughes argued that perception was all that counted. 'One thing that's been interesting this entire campaign season to watch is that people that say facts are facts. They're not really facts,' she said on NPR's *The Diane Rehm Show*. 'It's kind of like looking at ratings or looking at a glass of half-full water. Everybody has a way of interpreting them to be the truth or not true. There's no such thing, unfortunately, anymore as facts.'

But Conway was a senior White House official, not a media cheerleader. In a single sound bite, she had not only acknowledged the dawn of the Post-Truth era, but embraced it. In her sunny celebration of Spicer's intervention, she had given demotic form to Nietzsche's famous dictum that 'there are no facts, only interpretations'. NBC's reporter might regard Spicer's claim as a lie, but this, from her perspective, was to misunderstand the new rules of political debate. There was no stable, verifiable reality – only an endless battle to define it, your 'facts' versus my 'alternative facts'. The key was to keep ahead in that battle. Victory had always been at the heart of politics. But now – if Conway's maxim prevailed – it was the only thing of consequence.

It would be idle to deny the role that Trump's personal psychology and instincts have played in this process. Long before his presidential candidacy, the tycoon's relationship with the truth was frayed at best. From Roy Cohn, his lawyer, fixer and confidant – and former chief counsel to the McCarthy anti-communist hearings – he learned that 'brand' mattered more than the public ledger of fact and fiction, and that the sleepless quest for publicity was much more important than flawlessly objective coverage. What Cohn taught Trump was much more than old-school public relations – the management of news – but the creation of a modern myth. In this game, facts were a luxury and often an irrelevance.[9]

In his ghosted bestseller, *The Art of the Deal*, Trump referred approvingly to 'truthful hyperbole' – a euphemism if ever there was one. What mattered was not veracity, but impact. His butler, Anthony Senecal, has claimed that Trump once alleged that the tiles in the nursery at Mar-a-Lago, his West Palm Beach club, were personally made by Walt Disney. When Senecal questioned this unlikely tale, his boss replied: 'Who cares?'[10]

What Trump meant was that the story mattered more than the facts. And it was precisely upon this basis that he campaigned in 2016. Instead of force-feeding the electorate with an inventory of facts and the details of his résumé, he bellowed a narrative that imposed a crude sort of order upon the shifting complexities of modern life. He was explicitly divisive, promising a ban on Muslim immigration, a wall along the Mexican border, a return to economic protectionism.

But that was the whole point: to offer the great mass of white voters a series of enemies against whom they could unite, a story in which they could play a part, and a mythical plan to 'Make America Great Again'. The effect was narcotic rather than rational: better a fantasy narrative that felt good than none at all. At the heart of this narration stood Trump himself, a soiled Gatsby whose vulgar flashiness – much mocked in the media – was precisely what made the story so seductive.[11]

Victory persuaded him that he was now more or less liberated from the pesky constraints of fact. Scroll forward to Trump's first solo press conference as President, in which he claimed that he had achieved 'the biggest electoral college win since Ronald Reagan'. When corrected by NBC's Peter Alexander who pointed out that, in 2008, Obama had secured 365 votes – 61 more than Trump – the President muttered: 'I was talking about Republicans.' Alexander replied that George H. W. Bush had won 426 votes in 1988, and asked, on this basis of his phony claims, why Americans should trust him. Apparently unfazed, the President said only: 'I was given that information. I actually, I've seen that information around. But it was a very substantial victory, do you agree with that?'[12] In other words: who cares?

So it is tempting to ascribe the rise of Post-Truth to the rise of Trump. Tempting, and wrong. If this crisis of veracity could be blamed upon a single political sociopath, the problem would be containable and time-limited (no US President may serve more than two four-year terms). But Trump is more symptom than cause. He had been considering a run at the presidency for decades, and mocked accordingly. But, as he clearly intuited, in 2016 the stars suddenly aligned in his favour.

He also grasped that, *mutatis mutandis*, the decision of the British people to leave the European Union was a dress rehearsal for his own eventual victory. Days before the presidential election, he predicted that the result would be 'Brexit plus, plus, plus'.[13] What he meant was that the British insurgency against the pro-EU Establishment would be matched and surpassed by the American people's uprising against Washington's failed elites.

The parallels were much deeper, however. Arron Banks, the businessman who bankrolled the Leave.EU campaign, was correct in his analysis of the referendum outcome: 'The Remain campaign featured fact, fact, fact, fact. It just doesn't work. You've got to connect with people emotionally. It's the Trump success.'[14] Those pressing for Britain's continued EU membership bombarded the public with statistics: leaving would cost 950,000 UK jobs, the average wage would fall by £38 a week, each family would pay an average of £350 a year more on basic goods, £66 million a day invested by EU countries in the UK would be at risk, the cost of leaving would be £4,300 per household ... and so on, and so on.[15] It became easy to caricature this torrent of indigestible data as no more than a series of arbitrary claims.

What the Brexiteers understood was the need for simplicity and emotional resonance: a narrative that would give visceral meaning to a decision that might otherwise appear technical and abstract. As Dominic Cummings, campaign director of Vote Leave, argued at the time, the case for departure had to be clear and cleave to the specific grievances of the public. A message based upon the trade opportunities of Brexit – 'Go Global' –

might be intellectually defensible but it would not win votes. Earlier research by Cummings on Britain's potential membership of the euro had revealed the potential traction of a pledge to 'Take Back Control'.

Second, he believed that the weekly cost of EU membership – allegedly, £350 million – should be front and centre in the campaign and, crucially, identified as a dividend for the National Health Service. In other words: subsidise doctors and nurses, not Brussels bureaucrats. Third, the campaign should present the potential accession of Turkey to the EU as a clear and present danger to Britain's control of immigration policy. 'I was surprised at what a shock it was to IN [the Remain campaign] when we hit them with Turkey,' Cummings later recalled in a blogged memoir.[16] Surprised or not, he was right that the prospect of immigration – especially from Turkey – would swing many votes and help to sweep the Leave campaign to a historic victory.

The analogies with Trump's success are not exact but, as Banks understood, they are close enough. The speed with which the Brexiteers shifted their ground on the pledges which had won the referendum was breathtaking. On the BBC's *Newsnight*, the day after the vote, Daniel Hannan, a Conservative MEP, denied that his side had promised or insinuated that there would be a dramatic reduction in immigrant members. 'We never said there was going to be some radical decline,' he told the astonished presenter, Evan Davis. 'We want a measure of control.'[17]

Defending his personal position, Hannan subsequently declared: 'Chaps, look at what I said throughout the campaign: it's all on Twitter, YouTube etc. I was for more control, not for minimal immigration.'[18] This might have been true of Hannan personally – a politician known for his integrity and intellect – but it was disingenuous to claim that the winning side – the 'We' to which Hannan referred – had not encouraged the impression that the number of migrants entering the country would fall.

On 16 June, Nigel Farage, the then leader of the UK Independence Party, unveiled a poster of a huge queue of Syrian refugees under the slogan: 'Breaking Point'.[19] The image was widely disowned, not least by Boris Johnson, the official Leave campaign's most prominent spokesman, who declared himself 'profoundly unhappy with it'.[20] No doubt he was: the poster made explicit what others preferred only to insinuate.

The voters who had backed Brexit sought control *with a purpose*. In their different ways, the various Leave campaigns were content to unleash soaring expectations among those who chose to blame their misfortunes – real or imagined – upon immigrants. Thus was nurtured the pernicious notion that population mobility is a zero-sum game: that those who come to the UK are a bunch of freeloaders, depriving indigenous Britons of school places, housing, jobs and healthcare (all mythical claims, comprehensively debunked by Essex University's Neli Demireva).[21] Though Turkey's membership of the EU was a remote prospect at best – as the European Commission's latest annual report on its progress makes clear – it suited the Brexiteers to stoke fear of its accession and a consequent wave of Muslim migrants.[22]

This was Post-Truth politics at its purest – the triumph of the visceral over the rational, the deceptively simple over the honestly complex. There was no way that such expectations about immigration could ever be met by a government serious about economic growth. There would always be sectors in which skilled EU migrants were required – at the time of writing, 130,000 of them work in the British health- and social care system, and more are needed. The referendum result made no difference one way or the other to the rules governing immigration from outside the EU or to Britain's obligations under the UN Refugee Convention. The global forces driving population mobility would not be tamed by the UK's departure from one supranational organisation.

Britain was never going to become the nativist homeland that some imagined and been encouraged to imagine: it was always going to remain a pluralist, heterogeneous nation, welcoming many thousands of newcomers a month. But voters could be forgiven for believing otherwise.

No less spurious was the assertion – emblazoned on the side of the Leave battle bus – that Brexit would yield a £350 million weekly top-up for the cash-strapped NHS. For a start, the pledge did not take account of the rebate received by Britain: its net contribution per week to the EU was closer to £250 million.[23] Having pointed out the error, the UK Statistics Authority declared itself 'disappointed to note that there continue to be suggestions that the UK contributes £350 million to the EU each week, and that this full amount could be spent elsewhere'.[24] But the Leave campaign proceeded, unabashed. Cummings insists that Boris Johnson and his Leave colleague Michael Gove were 'agreed and determined' to spend this money on the health service. Perhaps they had convinced themselves that this magical cash transfer was going to happen: Post-Truth, as we shall see, is not the same as lying.

Other senior members of the Leave team were quite content to row back from the campaign's topline promise. Four days after the referendum, Chris Grayling, the then Leader of the House of Commons, downgraded it to 'an aspiration'.[25] Iain Duncan Smith, another prominent Brexiteer, also distanced himself from the hitherto unambiguous claim: 'I never said that during the course of the election [*sic*]. The £350m was an extrapolation of the £19.1bn – that's the total amount of money we gave across to the European Union. What we actually said was a significant amount of it would go to the NHS.'[26]

This was not, of course, what the voters had been led to expect every time they saw the Leave battle bus on television, or read the pinned tweet of the campaign's director, Matthew Elliott: 'Let's give our NHS the £350 million the EU takes every week.'[27]

When Chuka Umunna, a senior Labour MP, tabled an amendment to the legislation triggering Britain's exit negotiations that would have tested the impact of leaving upon the NHS, it was swept aside in the House of Commons. Cummings admits: 'Would we have won without £350m/NHS? All our research and the close result strongly suggests No.' But the speed with which the pledge was dumped suggests that it was never likely to be honoured. To borrow a distinction often made by Trump's supporters, it was evidently a mistake to take the Leave campaign literally rather than seriously.

Against this backdrop of broken or flimsy promises, you might expect enthusiasm for Brexit to collapse as the months passed and the scales fell. Not a bit of it. According to an Opinium survey published in January 2017, 52 per cent of voters believed that Britain 'made the right decision in deciding to leave the European Union'.[28] Some polls, it is true, reflected concerns about the likely content of the final deal. But, even as the Leave campaign's promises melted away, there was little sign of buyer's remorse. By February, support for the government's strategy had risen to 53 per cent, and 47 per cent said they thought Prime Minister Theresa

May would get the right deal for Britain (compared to only 29 per cent who believed she would fail).[29]

A similar pattern asserted itself in the first weeks of Trump's presidency: though he himself remained unpopular, the measures he had taken and promised commanded general support.[30] Which brings us to the very heart of the Post-Truth phenomenon.

TRUTH OUT, EMOTION IN

Lying has been an integral part of politics since early humans arranged themselves in tribes. Anthropologists note the importance of deception in primitive societies, especially, but not exclusively, when dealing with outsiders.[31] Plato ascribed to Socrates the notion of the 'noble lie' – a myth that inspires social harmony and civic devotion. In Chapter XVIII of *The Prince*, Machiavelli urges the ruler to be 'a great pretender and dissembler'.

To take the historic experience of America: its ideal of political truthfulness is itself rooted in a fiction. 'I cannot tell a lie,' George Washington is supposed to have said when confronted by his father over the fallen cherry tree. 'I did cut it with my hatchet.' But this parable was the invention of Parson Mason Locke Weems, Washington's mythographer – who, incidentally, claimed to be the rector of a church that did not exist.[32]

In American culture, the bookend to the young Washington's (confected) declaration was Richard

Nixon's claim in November 1973, 'I am not a crook.'[33] President Truman had previously described him pithily as 'a no good, lying bastard. He can lie out of both sides of his mouth at the same time, and if he ever caught himself telling the truth, he'd lie just to keep his hand in.'[34] Barry Goldwater, the defeated Republican candidate in the presidential contest of 1964, remembered him as 'the most dishonest individual I ever met in my life'.[35]

Nixon knew full well what awaited the politician who was caught lying. As he warned his aide, John Dean: 'If you are going to lie, you go to jail for the lie rather than the crime. So believe me, don't ever lie.'[36] But he did not anticipate the convulsion his misdeeds and falsehoods would cause the American polity. Watergate, as well as bequeathing a suffix to almost every subsequent scandal, drained a nation of faith in its political class, threatening the presidency itself, as well as bringing down an individual president.

The sunny likeability of Ronald Reagan was the escape hatch through which his party sought to exit the Nixon era once and for all. Yet Reagan himself was no stranger to falsehood. He claimed, for instance, to have helped the filming of the concentration camps and their liberation – whereas, in fact, he had not left the US during the Second World War. Even more famous is the form in which he finally admitted the substance of the Iran–Contra scandal: 'I told the American people I did not trade arms for hostages. My heart and my best intentions still tell me that is true, but the facts and the evidence tell me it is not.'[37] This gap between feeling and fact is relevant to our own era, as we shall see. Indeed, for the fortieth President there was no obvious reason to distinguish between the two. After correcting someone else's mistaken memory of meeting him when he was a young actor, Reagan offered this revealing consolation: 'You believed it because you wanted to believe it. There's nothing wrong with that. *I do it all the time*.'[38]

Such rationalisations might assuage the presidential conscience, but they did nothing to alleviate the culture of political suspicion that had its roots in Vietnam and Watergate and reached its apotheosis in the Monica Lewinsky affair and the subsequent impeachment of Bill Clinton. Asserting with grave intensity 'I did not have sexual relations with that woman', Clinton forever tarnished his own record and plunged the republic into a crisis that eroded what little trust remained in its politicians and condemned the US political system to apparently inescapable polarisation.[39]

For centuries, and certainly since the Enlightenment, it has been an unchallenged assumption that even the most robust democracy sustains damage when its politicians lie habitually. It was precisely because Tony Blair had presented himself – and been seen by voters – as 'a pretty straight sort of guy' that the controversy over his Iraq War dossiers caused him so much difficulty. To this day, Blair and his communications chief, Alastair Campbell, deny that these documents – the basis for Britain's participation in the conflict – were 'dodgy', 'sexed up' or otherwise falsified. Nonetheless, the pop-star politician of 1997 came to be perceived by many as 'Bliar', a corrosive force in British politics rather than the saviour of the Labour Party. 'There is this huge stuff about trust,'[40] noted Campbell in a diary entry in July 2003 – an astute, if bleak, observation about the predicament that all politicians of all parties were facing.

Yet political lies, spin and falsehood are emphatically not the same as Post-Truth. What is new is not the mendacity of politicians but the public's response to it. Outrage gives way to indifference and, finally, to collusion. Lying is regarded as the norm even in democracies – as it is in Poland, where the nationalist ruling party, Prawo i Sprawiedliwość (Law and Justice), has routinely disseminated falsehoods about homosexuals, refugees spreading disease and collaboration between communists and anti-communists.[41] We no longer expect our elected politicians to speak the truth: that, for now, has been written out of the job description, or at least significantly relegated on the list of required attributes.

This is familiar enough in societies scarred by past totalitarianism or present autocracy. In his excellent memoir of contemporary Russia, *Nothing Is True and Everything Is Possible,* Peter Pomerantsev describes the weariness that such assumptions breed:

> And when you go check (through friends, through
> Reuters, through anyone who isn't [state-controlled,
> pro-Putin channel] Ostankino) whether there really
> are fascists taking over Ukraine or whether there are
> children being crucified you find it's all untrue, and the
> women who said they saw it all are actually hired extras
> dressed up as 'eye-witnesses'. But even when you
> know the whole justification for the President's war is
> fabricated, even when you fathom that the reason is to
> create a new political technology to keep the President
> all-powerful and forget about the melting economy, even
> when you know and understand this the lies are told so
> often on Ostankino that after a while you find yourself
> nodding because it's hard to get your head around
> the idea that they are lying quite so much and quite
> so brazenly and all the time and at some level you feel
> that if Ostankino can lie so much and get away with it
> doesn't that mean that they have real power, a power to
> define what is true and what isn't, and wouldn't you do
> better just to nod anyway?⁴²

Sheer exhaustion can strip even the vigilant citizen of his or her commitment to truth. But what takes its place? In Putin's Russia, according to Pomerantsev, it is cognitive resignation, a withdrawal from an apparently unwinnable race. What matters is not rational deliberation but settled conviction. According to Alexander Dugin, the Russian political scientist and polemicist (nicknamed 'Putin's Rasputin'), 'truth is a matter of belief ... there is no such thing as facts'. It is surely no accident that Dugin has proved so influential among the American 'alt-Right' – the loose-knit network of nationalists that stretches from the White House office of Stephen Bannon, Trump's chief strategist, to neo-Nazis and survivalist groups.[43] They share with him a belief that truth is what you make of it.

In the West, it is emotional connection – always part of political decision-making – that threatens to eclipse our inherited insistence upon the truth as the main criterion in political contests. Michael Moore, the American documentary-maker and Left-wing activist, was one of the few commentators to predict the outcome of the presidential election. In his film *Michael Moore in Trumpland* he described the feelings that would drive voters to back the under-qualified Republican candidate:

> They've lost their jobs, the banks foreclosed, next came the divorce and now the wife and kids are gone, the car's been repo'ed. They haven't had a vacation in years, they're stuck with the shitty [healthcare] bronze plan where you can't even get a fucking Percocet. They've

essentially lost everything they have except one thing
[…]: the right to vote.

While the extent to which the support of the
'left-behind' and dispossessed accounted for Trump's
victory remains contentious, Moore was right to identify a resentful demand for change as the Republican
candidate's greatest ally. What the filmmaker grasped
was that the electorate was in no mood to hear about
Hillary Clinton's qualifications for the Oval Office
or, conversely, to pay much attention to those warning them of Trump's lies, bigotry and amateurism.
They wanted to send 'the biggest "fuck you" in human
history'. And, Moore continued, 'It will feel *good* – for
a day, or maybe a week. Possibly a month.'[44]

Trump was never a *sympathetic* candidate. The
opinion polls showed that the American people were
perfectly aware of his character flaws. But he communicated a brutal empathy to them, rooted not in
statistics, empiricism or meticulously acquired information, but an uninhibited talent for rage, impatience
and the attribution of blame. The assertion that he was
'plain-speaking' did not mean – as it might have in the
past – 'he is speaking the truth'. In 2016, it meant: 'this
candidate is different and might just address my anxieties and hopes.'

The sociologist Arlie Russell Hochschild has written
of the 'deep story' that underpins political attitudes and

social behaviour: 'A deep story is a feels-as-if story –
it's the story feelings tell, in the language of symbols.
It removes judgment. It removes fact. It tells us how
things feel.' In her travels around Louisiana's bayou
country, drawing upon many conversations, she exca-
vated one such story that, she said, shaped the way in
which those to whom she spoke saw and understood
modern America.

It was grounded in an elaborate metaphor: 'you are
patiently standing in a long line leading up a hill, as in
a pilgrimage. You are situated in the middle of this line,
along with others who are also white, older, Christian,
and predominantly male, some with college degrees,
some not.' Over the brow of the hill 'is the American
dream, the goal of everyone waiting in line'. But 'the
sun is hot and the line unmoving. In fact, is it moving
backward?' Your income is stagnant or falling. Employ-
ment is scarce where you live. And then: 'You see people
cutting in line ahead of you!' In Hochschild's account,
the men and women in the line feel that they have
followed the rules, have made their country great – and
yet are losing out to women, immigrants, public sector
workers, refugees and other beneficiaries of taxpayer's
money 'running through a liberal sympathy sieve'.[45]

Hochschild's research is not an apologia but a basis
for interpretation. The prism of the 'deep story' – in
this case, the story of the American Right in the South
– is an invaluable tool in the analysis of the Post-Truth

era. It explains the role played by narrative – as opposed
to disaggregated data – in political and social conduct.

This role is scarcely new. For most of human history,
shared mythologies and tribal stories have done more
to explain human behaviour than the cool assessment
of verifiable evidence. Every society has its founding
legends that bind it together, shape its moral bound-
aries and inhabit its dreams of the future. Since the
Scientific Revolution and the Enlightenment, however,
these collective narratives have competed with rationality, pluralism and the priority of truth as a basis for
social organisation.

What *is* new is the extent to which, in the new
setting of digitalisation and global interconnected-
ness, emotion is reclaiming its primacy and truth is in
retreat. The forces driving this retreat are the subject
of the next chapter. But the resurgence of emotional
narrative in recent decades – its renewed centrality – is
the essential corollary.

If the twentieth century was the age of totalitarianism
and its ignominious defeat, it was also the age of therapy
and its robust survival. Sigmund Freud reframed the way
in which humanity is seen and – irrespective of academic
vogue – introduced to the popular bloodstream a
series of ideas that have proved remarkably resilient. In
psychoanalysis, claims and counter-claims are assessed
pathologically, in reference to personal neuroses, rather
than forensically, according to traditional notions of

truth and falsehood. The imperative is to treat the patient successfully, not to establish facts.

Confined to the consulting room, this was initially an entirely private matter. But the paradigm of therapy has spread far beyond this clinical setting, to assume a dominant role in contemporary culture and mores. Long before 'memes' were said to go 'viral', popular psychology had spread around the globe and lodged itself in the demotic as a means of explaining everything.

The forms that this conquest has taken range from genuinely illuminating insights into the way we live, to rampant psychobabble that excuses everything and explains nothing. An example of the former category is the school of behavioural economics that has shed fascinating light upon the role of psychological and social impulses in economic decisions.[46] Closely related to this is the study of 'emotional intelligence' – popularised by the psychologist Daniel Goleman – and of the role played by emotional competencies such as empathy, self-awareness, and self-regulation in leadership, workplace performance and social relations.[47] Building upon these insights, Drew Westen and Daniel Pink have explored, respectively, the role of emotion in political behaviour and the growing importance of the right hemisphere of the brain – responsible for creativity, inventiveness and empathy – in an age of automation.[48]

As emancipating as the greater understanding of emotion and psychological impulses has undoubtedly been, it has also reset the rules of the human game in ways that are not always constructive. The legendary psychologist Bruno Bettelheim, a serial fabricator about his own past, please note, gave modernity one of its most pernicious texts in hailing 'the need and usefulness of acting on the basis of fictions that are known to be false'.[49]

According to this dictum, emotional necessity trumps strict adherence to the truth. Those who quibble are no better than Thomas Gradgrind in Dickens's *Hard Times* and his dreary demand: 'Now, what I want is Facts. Teach these boys and girls nothing but Facts. Facts alone are wanted in life.' No: the higher purpose of humankind is to escape literalism and to shape one's own reality.

It is not hard to see how self-serving this axiom might become. As David Brooks notes in his book on the baby boomers – those born between the end of the Second World War and the mid-sixties – that generation is 'relatively unmoved by lies or transgressions that don't seem to do anyone obvious harm. They prize good intentions and are willing to tolerate a lot from people whose hearts are in the right place.'[50] They embellish their military records, résumés and sexual histories.[51] For this cohort, emotional sincerity has always been the highest virtue – greater, in many instances, than the starchy pursuit of objective truth urged upon them by their parents.

It is not that honesty is dead: what psychologists call 'truth bias' remains a fundamental component of human character. But it is now perceived as one priority among many, and not necessarily the highest. Sharing your innermost feelings, shaping your life-drama, speaking from the heart: these pursuits are increasingly in open competition with traditional forensic values. As Ralph Keyes, one of the first writers to send up a warning flare about the perils of Post-Truth, puts it, many 'have adopted a therapeutic posture in which no one is held accountable for dishonesty, or much of anything'.[52]

The risk is that an ever-greater proportion of judgements and decisions will be banished to the realm of feeling, that the quest for truth will become a branch of emotional psychology, without moorings or foundations. The question, then, is how the ideal of veracity became so weakened, so etiolated, that it competes so poorly with contemporary emotionalism. Whatever happened to truth?

2

'YOU CAN'T HANDLE THE TRUTH!': THE ORIGINS OF THE POST-TRUTH ERA

THE COLLAPSE OF TRUST

'People in this country have had enough of experts': the assertion was striking not only because of its audacity, but because of the person making it. Michael Gove, the then Justice Secretary, was one of the most intellectual members of David Cameron's Cabinet, formidably articulate, cultured and erudite. Of all the senior champions of Brexit, he was the last person one would have expected to attack 'experts'. But this was precisely what he did in a question and answer session on the EU referendum broadcast by Sky News on 3 June 2016.

Months after the vote was won, Gove would tell the BBC's Andrew Marr that the reports of his remark had been 'unfair', that it was 'manifestly nonsense' to suggest that all experts were wrong, and that he had been referring to 'a sub-class of experts, particularly economists, pollsters, social scientists, who really do need to reflect on some of the mistakes that they've made in the same way as a politician I've reflected on some of the mistakes that I've made.'[1]

Entitled as he was to offer this *ex post facto* clarification, Gove's original attack had been – as he surely knew – politically canny. It tapped into a seam of distrust that was essential to Leave's victory; a growing suspicion that traditional sources of authority and information were unreliable, self-interested or even downright fraudulent. The Brussels elite was not the only hierarchy or institution against which Britons rose up in anger in the referendum.

This collapse of trust is the social basis of the Post-Truth era: all else flows from this single, poisonous source. To put it another way, all successful societies rely upon a relatively high degree of honesty to preserve order, uphold the law, hold the powerful to account and generate prosperity. As Francis Fukuyama observes in his book *Trust*, the social capital that accrues when citizens cooperate sincerely and scrupulously translates into economic success and lowers the cost of litigation, regulation and contractual enforcement.[2]

Beyond the commercial sphere, trust is an essential human survival mechanism, the basis of co-existence that permits any human relationship, from marriage to a complex society, to work with any degree of success. In the nineties, Ted Goertzel, a sociologist at Rutgers University, conducted a telephone poll that found that those inclined to be suspicious of others were also more likely to believe conspiracy theories.[3] A community without trust ultimately becomes no more than an atomised collection of individuals, trembling in their stockades.

Yet that is precisely the trajectory upon which the world has been embarked in recent decades, as an unrelenting series of storms have conspired to deplete what reserves of trust remain. The financial crisis of 2008 took the global economy to the brink of meltdown, averted only by eye-wateringly huge state bailouts for the very banks that were responsible for the disastrous collapse. Occupy Wall Street was only the most visible manifestation of a much broader disgust that some institutions were evidently 'too big to fail', while ordinary people paid the price in the subsequent recession and cuts to public services imposed by governments conscious of deficit.

Hostility to the globalised economy shifted from the fringes to the centre of political discourse. It became commonplace to question an economic system initially presented as a reliable source of rising prosperity that now seemed horribly vulnerable to the caprice of its operating elite and – perhaps worse – rigged to benefit that same tiny group while living standards stagnated or fell for the remaining 99 per cent. Statistical counter-claims in support of globalisation mostly compounded the outrage. The numbers advanced in defence of the system did not *feel* right.[4]

In Britain, the financial crisis was followed by the humiliation of the political class in the 2009 parliamentary expenses scandal. In a series of remarkable articles, the *Daily Telegraph* exposed the sharp practices that enabled MPs to supplement their official salary by charging the taxpayer for everything from moat-clearing and a £1,600 duck house to a bath plug and pornographic films.

Politicians had long been objects of suspicion. But the allegations of 'sleaze' against the Conservatives in the nineties and the charge that the Labour government of 1997–2010 was all 'spin' and no substance were but a dry run for this extraordinary national spectacle – part-comedy, part-tragedy. In 1986, only 38 per cent said that they trusted governments 'to place the needs of the nation above the interests of their own political party'. By 2014 that figure had fallen to about 18 per cent. The rot was now threatening the whole democratic process.

Meanwhile, scandals in show business – especially the monstrous sexual crimes of Jimmy Savile – have dragged the BBC and other institutions through the mire. Without hyperbole, the broadcaster's much-admired World Affairs Editor, John Simpson, described the Savile affair as the BBC's 'worst crisis' in fifty years. As became horribly clear, the late *Top of the Pops* presenter had been the beneficiary of a culture of institutional neglect: what James Q. Wilson in his classic book *Bureaucracy* calls the problem of 'selective attention'. Blind eyes were turned, inquiries were token, shoulders were shrugged. Whatever anxieties BBC staff felt, most of them did not report them. Paradoxically, Savile's access to Broadmoor secure hospital and Duncroft Approved School for Girls was seen as evidence of his charitable instinct rather than something truly ghastly. Savile was certainly protected by stardom and his notorious readiness to threaten litigation. But he also depended upon the indifference of others. Yet again, in the eyes of the public, a great institution had been found wanting.

For print journalism, the hacking controversy was no less a disaster, forcing the closure of the *News of the World*, the resignation of its former editor, Andy Coulson, as Number Ten's director of communications, and Lord Leveson's sweeping inquiry of 2011–12 into the conduct of the press. At the time of writing, the regulatory regime to which British publications will submit themselves is still unresolved. But much more is at stake here than the precise (and varying) rules to which the press will be subject.

In 2003, the disclosure by the *New York Times* that one of its reporters, Jayson Blair, had falsified or plagiarised content in 673 articles over the course of four years forced the paper to publish a 14,000-word review of his misconduct. This was not just a lapse in editorial control and judgement. The debacle represented a mortal threat – narrowly averted – to one of the great institutions of American civic life. It is surely no accident that President Trump routinely tweets that the *New York Times* is 'failing': he knows which media organisations to target – the 'halo brands' – and which will seek to hold him truly accountable. For all the talk of the 'dead tree press', it was the *Washington Post* that forced the President to sack his National Security Adviser, Michael Flynn, after only twenty-four days.

Likewise, the trauma of the British hacking scandal – compounded by the financial difficulties of printed media in the digital era – has imperilled public trust in the very journalism that is needed more than ever. The task of populism is to simplify at all costs, to squeeze inconvenient facts into a preordained shape, or exclude them altogether. The task of journalism is to reveal the complexity, nuance and paradox of public life, as well as to ferret out wrongdoing and, most important of all, to water the roots of democracy with a steady supply of reliable news. Precisely when trust in the media is required most it has, according to global opinion polls, fallen to an all-time low.[5]

We live in an age of institutional fragility. A society's institutions act as guard rails, the bodies that incarnate its values and continuities. To shine a bright light on their failures, decadence and outright collapse is intrinsically unsettling. But that is not all. Post-Truth has flourished in this context, as the firewalls and antibodies (to mix metaphors) have weakened. When the putative guarantors of honesty falter, so does truth itself. The philosopher A. C. Grayling may well be right to identify the financial crisis as the germinal moment that led in a matter of years to the Post-Truth era. 'The world changed after 2008,' he told the BBC in January 2017 – and so it did.[6]

THE RISE OF THE MISINFORMATION INDUSTRY

If institutional failure has eroded the primacy of truth, so too has the multi-billion-dollar industry of misinformation, false propaganda and phony science that has arisen in recent years. Just as Post-Truth is not simply another name for lying, this industry has nothing to do with legitimate lobbying and corporate relations. Businesses, charities, campaigning bodies and public figures are perfectly entitled to seek professional representation in the maze of government and media. This is all part of the rough and tumble of policymaking, consultation and publicity, and no threat to a healthy civic structure.

Quite separate, however, is the systematic spread of falsehood by front organisations acting on behalf of vested interests that wish to suppress accurate information or to prevent others acting upon it.[7] As the campaigning journalist Ari Rabin-Havt has put it: 'These lies are part of a coordinated, strategic assault designed to hide the truth, confuse the public, and create controversy where none previously existed.'[8]

This assault has its distant roots in the launch of the Tobacco Industry Research Committee in 1954, a corporate-sponsored body set up in response to growing public anxiety over the connection between smoking and lung disease. What made the committee so significant was the subtlety of its objective. It sought not to win the battle outright, but to dispute the existence of a scientific consensus. It was designed to sabotage public confidence and establish a false equivalence between those scientists who detected a link between tobacco use and lung cancer and those who challenged them. The objective was not academic victory but popular confusion. As long as doubt hovered over the case against tobacco, the lucrative status quo was safe.

This provided climate change deniers with a model for their own campaigns. Marc Morano, the former Republican aide who runs the website ClimateDepot. com, has described gridlock as 'the greatest friend a global warming skeptic has because that's all you really want … We're the negative force. We're just trying to stop stuff.' Foreshadowing Gove's attack on 'experts', Morano has conceded that the ideologically driven layman is often at an advantage when taking on a scholar: 'You go up against a scientist, most of them are going to be in their own policy wonk world or area of expertise ... very arcane, very hard to understand, hard to explain, and very boorrring.'[9]

It follows that the trick is to provide disruptive entertainment as a distraction from plodding science. The media, especially twenty-four-hour news channels, are constantly hungry for confrontation, which often creates the illusion of a contest between equally legitimate positions – what Kingsley Amis called 'pernicious neutrality'.[10] A rolling dispute of this sort was certainly the objective of those behind 'Climategate': the disclosure in 2009 of thousands of emails and files hacked from a server at the University of East Anglia's Climate Research Unit. The brilliance of those reporting on the cache was to select phrases and sentences that appeared, collectively, to suggest an academic cover-up, and a humiliating gap between what the scientists claimed in public and what they said to one another in private.

As embarrassing as the emails undoubtedly were – revealing moments of exasperation and frustration – they did not, as was routinely claimed, undermine the science of climate change. To take an example: in one message, Dr Kevin Trenberth, an MIT scientist, wrote: 'We cannot account for the lack of warming at the moment, and it is a travesty that we can't.' A clear enough admission, surely? Not so, as it transpired. The 'travesty' to which Trenberth was actually referring was the absence of 'an observing system adequate to track [climate change]'. He was not in any sense retracting his scientific conclusions about global warming but regretting a shortfall in the infrastructure that he and his colleagues needed.[11]

Report after report – by Penn State University, a UK parliamentary committee, the National Oceanic and Atmospheric Administration Inspector General's Office, fact-checking sites and an independent inquiry commissioned by UEA itself – found that the files did not undermine the scientific consensus on climate change, or impugn the academic integrity of the scientists involved.

But the deniers' work was already done. According to a survey by Yale University, public support for global warming science fell from 71 to 57 per cent between 2008 and 2010. A more recent UK poll, published in January 2017, suggested that 64 per cent of British adults believe that the climate is changing, 'primarily due to human activity'. This might seem like a reasonable majority. But consider the stakes: eleven years after the UK government's publication of the official Stern Review on the Economics of Climate Change, and nine since the Climate Change Act put emission reduction targets into law, the public is still not overwhelmingly persuaded that the very survival of humanity is at risk.

Before his election, Trump tweeted that the 'concept of global warming was created by and for the Chinese in order to make US manufacturing non-competitive'. Since taking office, he has surrounded himself with climate change sceptics. The principal objective of the deniers – to maintain the status quo – has never faced better odds.

Their insight, shared by the opponents of healthcare reform in the US, is that evidence-based public policy can be undermined by the alignment of well-crafted propaganda and ideological predisposition. In the case of 'Obamacare', it was the myth of 'death panels' that achieved this goal. In a Facebook post in August 2009, Sarah Palin, the former Governor of Alaska, claimed that, if Obama's affordable care proposals were enacted, bureaucratic review bodies would decide whether elderly patients or children with chronic conditions were 'worthy of medical care'.

This was a grotesque distortion of the bill's proposal to offer voluntary counselling to Medicare patients on living wills, end-of-life care and palliative treatment. There were no plans for 'death panels' and never had been. But the phrase had deep emotional and ideo-logical resonance with those predisposed to distrust healthcare reform and to interpret it as an un-American, proto-socialist measure. A week after Palin's post, almost

90 per cent of Americans were aware of her warning, and three out of ten said that they believed it. Once again, the lie prevailed. Even though the eventual legislation omitted the grossly misrepresented counselling clause, the number of Americans anxious about death panels had *risen* by August 2012.[12]

These campaigns of disinformation have paved the way for the Post-Truth era. Their purpose is invariably to sow doubt rather than to triumph outright in the court of public opinion (usually an impractical objective). As the institutions that traditionally act as social arbiters – referees on the pitch, as it were – have been progressively discredited, so well-funded pressure groups have encouraged the public to question the existence of conclusively reliable truth. Accordingly, the normal practice of adversarial debate is morphing into an unhealthy relativism, in which the epistemological chase is not only better than the catch – but all that matters. The point is simply to keep the argument going, to ensure that it never reaches a conclusion.

WELCOME TO THE DIGITAL BAZAAR

The rise of this treacherous industry has coincided with the wholesale metamorphosis of the media landscape and the digital revolution. In the first decade of the century, the ready availability of high-speed broadband transformed the Internet from the cheapest, fastest means of publication ever invented into something that would have a much more profound cultural, behavioural and philosophical impact.

What became known as 'Web 2.0' was not simply a technological phenomenon: it replaced hierarchies with 'peer-to-peer' recommendation, deference with collaboration, scheduled meetings with 'smartmobs', proprietary information with open-source software, and passive consumption of electronic media with user-generated content. It promised democratisation on an unprecedented scale.[13]

And, in a great many respects, it has delivered. Fashionable denigration of the digital revolution ignores the astonishing benefits it has brought to humanity in a matter of years. It is already hard to imagine a world without smartphones, Google, Facebook or YouTube, or to envisage (for instance) hospitals, schools, universities, aid agencies, charities or the service economy suddenly stripped of these tools. The connective tissue of the web is one of the greatest achievements in the history of human innovation. The only thing more remarkable than the impact of this technology is the speed with which we have come to take it for granted.

Yet, like all transformative innovations, the web holds a mirror up to humanity. Alongside its many merits it has also enabled and enhanced the worst of mankind's instincts, acting as a university for terrorists and a haven for con men.

Meanwhile, the same tech giants that have provided the stage, scenery and props for this thrilling global drama have become the beneficiaries of unprecedented amounts of information about its billions of players: so-called 'big data'. Between them, Google, Microsoft, Apple, Facebook and Amazon – the 'Big Five' – outstrip by a huge margin all the databanks, filing systems and libraries that have existed in human history. In every interaction, post, purchase or search, users reveal something more about themselves – information that has become the most valuable commodity in the world.

Gone, too, are the days when aggregating data was a wearisome human task. Software such as the open-source programming framework Hadoop and Google's MapReduce are able to crunch extraordinary quantities of data for any imaginable purpose. Many of these will be benign – the early identification of epidemics, for instance, based on search patterns. But the potential use of big data to manipulate financial markets and the political process is only now becoming clear.

As Sir Tim Berners-Lee, the founder of the World Wide Web, warned in his letter to mark its twenty-eighth birthday:

The current business model for many websites offers free content in exchange for personal data. Many of us agree to this – albeit often by accepting long and confusing terms and conditions documents – but

fundamentally we do not mind some information being
collected in exchange for free services. But, we're
missing a trick. As our data is then held in proprietary
silos, out of sight to us, we lose out on the benefits we
could realise if we had direct control over this data,
and chose when and with whom to share it. What's
more, we often do not have any way of feeding back to
companies what data we'd rather not share – especially
with third parties – the T&Cs [terms and conditions] are
all or nothing.[14]

The language was restrained, but the point was clear.
The web is at risk of becoming – may already have
become – a runaway train, crashing through privacy,
democratic norms and financial regulation.

This technology has also been the all-important,
primary, indispensable engine of Post-Truth. In the
first years of Web 2.0, it was optimistically assumed
by many that the Internet would inevitably smooth
the path to sustainable cooperation and pluralism. In
practice, the new technology has done at least as much
to foster online huddling and a general retreat into
echo chambers. As Barack Obama put it in his fare-
well address in January 2017: 'We become so secure in
our bubbles that we start accepting only information,
whether it's true or not, that fits our opinions, instead of
basing our opinions on the evidence that is out there.'
For all its wonders, the web tends to amplify the shrill

and to dismiss complexity. For many – perhaps most – it encourages confirmation bias rather than a quest for accurate disclosure.

In his book on truth, the late philosopher Bernard Williams characterised the Internet thus:

> [It] supports that mainstay of all villages, gossip. It constructs proliferating meeting places for the free and unstructured exchange of messages which bear a variety of claims, fancies and suspicions, entertaining, superstitious, scandalous, or malign. The chances that many of these messages will be true are low, and the probability that the system itself will help anyone to pick out the true ones is even lower.[15]

As we shall see in a later chapter, this prophecy, made in 2002, underestimated the web's growing capacity for self-correction. But its warning of online cantonisation has been comprehensively vindicated.

As in other respects, digital technology puts rocket boosters under existing instincts. One such is the tendency towards 'homophilous sorting'[16] – our impulse to congregate with the like-minded. To an extent, this impulse has always dictated our media consumption: in the UK, right-of-centre readers have long gravitated to the *Daily Telegraph*, while the liberal-Left favours the *Guardian*. But both newspapers have also been regarded as reliable providers of well-sourced news and accurate reporting. As C. P. Scott, editor of what was then the *Manchester Guardian* from 1872 to 1929, famously declared: 'Comment is free, but facts are sacred'.

Still broadly respected as a core principle by the mainstream quality press, Scott's distinction has been lost in the online miasma. Social media and search engines, with their algorithms and hashtags, tend to drive us towards content that we will like and people who agree with us. Too often we dismiss as 'trolls' those who dare to dissent. The consequence is that opinions tend to be reinforced and falsehoods unchallenged. We languish in the so-called 'filter bubble'.

Indeed, there has never been a faster or more powerful way to propagate a lie than to post it online. Russian propagandists pioneered many of the techniques of contemporary information manipulation, pouring out material through state sources, but also carefully orchestrated leaks made to resemble the work of independent cyber-punks. The impact of Russian hacking upon the 2016 American presidential election is still a matter of inquiry. But its extent is scarcely in doubt. If politics is war by other means, so too is information.[17]

FAKE NEWS

Post-Truth sells, too. Those whom the Columbia University professor Tim Wu has called the 'attention merchants' compete for our time – and market it as a hugely valuable product. They will go to almost any lengths to distract and engage us. They understand that William James was right: 'My experience is what I agree to attend to.'[18]

It follows that there are profits to be made from the production line of clickbait hoaxes – unscientific medical claims, crackpot theories, fictional sightings of UFOs or Jesus. The disincentives to publication are (to date) marginal, and the ease of production enticing. For those on social media, anonymity dramatically reduces accountability. The buzz of the hive sends the falsehood fizzing into cyberspace to do its work. Never has the old adage that a lie can travel halfway around the world while the truth is putting on its shoes seemed so timely.

As Eric S. Raymond famously predicted, the Cathedral is yielding place to the Bazaar.[19] Hierarchical systems of information in which established brands – newspapers, television channels – decide what news is fit for consumption struggle to compete with the cosmic Speakers' Corner of new media. It is a mistake to give up on the great MSM brands: the BBC, CNN, *The Times* (and its New York counterpart), the *Guardian*, the *Financial Times* and *The Economist* – to name but a handful – remain central to mainstream culture and discourse. But it is equally true that the established media face a fundamental challenge as they search for new business models that will enable them to stay true to their principles.

In the consequent cacophony, the flow of information is increasingly dominated by peer-to-peer interaction rather than the imprimatur of the traditional press. We consume what we already like, and shy away from the unfamiliar. The ultimate generator of novelty has also become the curator of hearsay, folklore and prejudice.

This, it should be emphasised, is not a design flaw. It is what the algorithms are meant to do: to connect us with the things we like, or might like. They are fantastically responsive to personal taste and – to date – fantastically blind to veracity. The web is the definitive vector of Post-Truth precisely because it is indifferent to falsehood, honesty and the difference between the two.

This is why 'fake news' has become such an issue, especially on Facebook. Among the most-read hoax stories of 2016 were the following: the claim that Obama had banned the Pledge of Allegiance in schools; 'Pope Francis Shocks World, Endorses Donald Trump for President, Releases Statement'; a report that Trump was 'Offering Free One-Way Tickets to Africa & Mexico for Those Who Wanna Leave America'; and 'ISIS Leader Calls for American Muslim Voters to Support Hillary Clinton'. Automated news feeds caused hundreds of thousands to read on Facebook that Fox News had fired one of its anchors, Megyn Kelly, for being a 'traitor'.[20]

As ludicrous as these stories may seem, they command belief: in December 2016, an Ipsos poll for BuzzFeed of more than 3,000 Americans found that 75 per cent of those who saw fake news headlines judged them to be accurate. On average, supporters of Hillary Clinton considered 58 per cent of familiar fake news headlines to be true, versus 86 per cent for Trump voters.[21] Much worse, a phony report alleging that Clinton was at the heart of a paedophile conspiracy persuaded twenty-eight-year-old Edgar Maddison Welch from Salisbury, North Carolina, to 'self-investigate' the ludicrous claims by firing shots from an assault rifle in a Washington, DC, pizza parlour.

The restaurant, Comet Ping Pong, had been falsely associated with the story, itself comprehensively debunked before Welch's attack. Death threats were received by the owner and staff, unwitting victims of the so-called 'Pizzagate' allegations.[22] It is worth noting that Michael Flynn, briefly Trump's National Security Adviser, had tweeted that the stories connecting Clinton with 'Sex crimes w/Children' were a 'MUST READ'. As tempting as it is to dismiss fake news as the staple diet of the fringe, it has enthusiastic consumers at the very apex of power.

All that matters is that the stories *feel* true; that they resonate. In politics, the pioneer of this doctrine was the administration of George W. Bush. As Ron Suskind reported in the *New York Times Magazine* in 2004, one of the President's aides – widely believed to be Karl Rove – told him that his journalistic methods were lamentably outdated:

The aide said that guys like me were 'in what we call the reality-based community', which he defined as people who 'believe that solutions emerge from your judicious study of discernible reality'. ... 'That's not the way the world really works anymore', he continued. 'We're an empire now, and when we act, we create our own reality. And while you're studying that reality – judiciously, as you will – we'll act again, creating other new realities, which you can study too, and that's how things will sort out. We're history's actors ... and you, all of you, will be left to just study what we do'.[23]

In other words: what reporters call reality is absolutely fungible. Those who have a platform to offer what Kellyanne Conway more recently called 'alternative facts' will do so. Step aside, and enjoy the ride.

As in politics, so in television. No genre has been more ironically named than 'reality TV'. Far from documenting the truth of everyday life, these shows have catapulted their participants into mostly scripted (or at least well-plotted) scenarios that present a preordained narrative as authentic behaviour. Some programmes – *Operation Repo, Amish Mafia* – offer disclaimers explaining that the content is a dramatised re-enactment of supposedly real incidents. Others – *The Bachelor, Jersey Shore, Duck Dynasty* – have been shown to be wholly or partly staged. Yet such disclosures have done nothing to reduce audience demand for these shows. The intensity of the drama, rather than its accuracy, is what matters. For the viewers, reality and entertainment have become coterminous.

This is the defining characteristic of the Post-Truth world. The point is not to determine the truth by a process of rational evaluation, assessment and conclusion. You choose your own reality, as if from a buffet. You also select your own falsehood, no less arbitrarily. In a classic instance of what psychologists call 'mirroring', Trump – notorious during the campaign for his falsehoods – began accusing his media critics of peddling 'fake news' themselves. Incandescent about reports by BuzzFeed and CNN that the Russian government was in a position to blackmail him, the President-elect refused to take a question from the cable channel's reporter during a press conference at Trump Tower in New York. His reasoning was straightforward. 'Not you,' he told Jim Acosta, CNN's senior White House correspondent. 'Your organization is terrible.' Acosta asked that he 'give us a chance'. But Trump was adamant: 'I'm not going to give you a question. You are fake news.'[24]

As President, he has made similar accusations on a regular basis. On 10 February 2017, he tweeted in response to a *New York Times* report about his lack of contact with the Chinese President, Xi Jinping: 'The failing @nytimes does major FAKE NEWS China story saying "Mr. Xi has not spoken to Mr. Trump since Nov.14." We spoke at length yesterday!' This tweet was itself fake news. At the time of the paper's initial report, the President had indeed not spoken to Xi since November. The story was updated when the White House reported the telephone call between the two leaders. But that did not stop Trump from unleashing his furious accusation.

At his first solo press conference as President six days later, he warmed to his theme. 'Many of our nation's reporters and folks will not tell you the truth and will not treat the wonderful people of our country with the respect that we deserve,' he said in his opening statement. 'Unfortunately, much of the media in Washington, DC, along with New York, Los Angeles in particular, speaks not for the people but for the special interests and for those profiting off a very, very obviously broken system.'

As aggressive as this was, it observed – just about – the normal rules of engagement of a president at odds with the media. The same could not be said, however, of his garbled remarks about leaks from his administration and their truth: 'The leaks are real; you're the one that wrote about them and reported them. The leaks are absolutely real ... The news is fake because so much of the news is fake.' Inasmuch as this meant anything, it was that the sources of the stories were authentic – but the reports were nonetheless fake. Truly, we were through the looking-glass.[25]

If digital technology is the hardware, Post-Truth has proven to be a mighty software. It reduces political discourse to a video game in which endless play, on multiple levels, is the sole point of the exercise. When Trump tweeted that the 'FAKE NEWS media' was the 'enemy of the people', he was not only borrowing from the traditional lexicon of autocracy. He was urging American citizens to behave like gamers, pick up their consoles and zero in on the bad guys carrying notepads. This is all about picking teams, intensity of feeling and escalating insults. It is the politics of pure spectacle.

It cannot be emphasised enough that this is not the familiar adversarial practice of a healthy democracy. Parliamentary systems depend upon confrontation across the Despatch Box. Legal structures pit advocates against one another, or enable an inquisitorial judge to cross-examine all participants in a case. Oliver Wendell Holmes argued that 'the best test of truth is the power of the thought to get itself accepted in the competition of the market, and that truth is the only ground upon which [men's] wishes safely can be carried out.'[26] But there is a difference between a structured marketplace of ideas, and a babel of shrieking voices in which anything goes and common ground not only shrinks but is positively shirked.

As Charlie Sykes, the conservative talk-show host and editor of *Right Wisconsin*, told *The Economist*: 'We've basically eliminated any of the referees, the gatekeepers

… There is nobody: you can't go to anybody and say: "Look, here are the facts".[27] Those responsible for the numerous fact checking sites that have arisen in recent years would doubtless protest. But, thus far, they have proven an inadequate force of resistance against the torrential outpourings of social media. When anyone with a Twitter account can claim to be a news source, it becomes infinitely harder to distinguish between fact and falsehood. Everyone and no one is an 'expert'.

Who can monitor a limitless space? Where are the Kitemarks, the watchdogs, the editorial forces sufficient to this task? As news consumption migrates from print and television to the online ether, this is no longer an academic question.

It is also, primarily, a question about *us*. As noted in the previous chapter, the clinching factor in the rise of Post-Truth has been our behaviour as citizens. By rewarding those who lie with political success, exempting them from the traditional expectations of integrity, we have seceded from the duties of citizenship. To the bellowed charge of Jack Nicholson's character in *A Few Good Men* – 'You can't handle the truth!' – we have no ready answer.

Surprise, pleasure, recognition and indignation are fundamental to the human experience: but they are an insufficient basis upon which to base our versions of reality. We retweet, give in to clickbait, share without due diligence. And this is often fun. But it is not without consequence, as the prankster culture of social media often suggests. We have conspired, unwittingly or otherwise, in the devaluation of truth by hibernating in the Hobbit hole of received opinion, our faces flickering from the light of countless electronic signals that reinforce what we already think we know. Fool's licence is meaningless when we are all fools.

3

CONSPIRACY AND DENIAL: THE FRIENDS OF POST-TRUTH

PARANOIA TAKES CENTRE STAGE

In November 1964, *Harper's Magazine* published a seminal article by the Columbia University professor of history Richard Hofstadter, entitled 'The Paranoid Style in American Politics'.[1] To this day, his essay remains the urtext for all who study modern conspiracy theories and their impact upon perceptions of truth.

Hofstadter's principal insight – abetted by his eloquence – was the distinction he drew between the paranoia of contemporary conspiracists and the scaremongering of those in centuries past who had aimed their fire at (for instance) Catholics, Masons and the Bavarian Illuminati:

> The spokesmen of those earlier movements felt that they stood for causes and personal types that were still in possession of their country – that they were fending off threats to a still established way of life. But the modern right wing … feels dispossessed: America has been largely taken away from them and their kind, though they are determined to try to repossess it and to prevent the final destructive act of subversion.

To 'Make America Great Again', one might say. But, Hofstadter continued, the conspiracists of his own time – principally, but not only, anti-communists and the heirs of McCarthy – believed themselves engaged in a millennial struggle that would determine much more than the fate of a single nation:

> The paranoid spokesman sees the fate of conspiracy in apocalyptic terms – he traffics in the birth and death of whole worlds, whole political orders, whole systems of human values. He is always manning the barricades of civilization. He constantly lives at a turning point. Like religious millennialists he expresses the anxiety of those who are living through the last days and he is sometimes disposed to set a date for the apocalypse.

Half a century later, Hofstadter's article remains an invaluable guide, except in one crucial respect. Conspiracy theories, he claimed, were 'a persistent psychic phenomenon, more or less constantly affecting a modest minority of the population'. But, in the Post-Truth era, this is no longer so.

Consider the case of Alex Jones, the Texas-based host of Infowars.com, who claims inter alia that the Sandy Hook massacre of 2012, in which twenty children died, was a hoax; that wicked genetic engineers are breeding human-fish hybrids; and that a vampiric elite, including the Clintons, is engaged in satanic child abuse. According to Jones, his conspiracist outbursts are heard by five million radio listeners every day and achieve eighty million video views a month. These statistics are hard to substantiate, but there is no doubt that Jones's reach is wide – and now high. Trump has appeared on his show, described his reputation as 'amazing', and reportedly called Jones after the election to thank him for his support ('he needs me,' according to the presenter). The White House has not denied that the two men remain in contact.[2]

In the past, a man like Jones would have worn a sandwich board and yelled at passers-by in the street. Now he has access to the most powerful politician in the world. What is so important to recognise is that this reflects a structural change as well as an unfortunate personal affinity between two braggarts. Both

Jones and Trump are part of a continuum that stretches from talk radio studios via sites such as Breitbart.com ('the platform for the alt-Right', according to its former executive chair, Stephen Bannon) to the Oval Office, a global nexus that has very little in common with the social arrangements of the past.

The last century bequeathed to us a system of gradually evolving, rules-based institutions, a hierarchy of knowledge and authority, in which representative bodies interacted with the state according to tried and tested protocols. That structure is now being challenged by a lattice of networks, connected not by institutional bonds but by the viral power of social media, cyberspace and sites that revel in their loathing of the MSM. The web has abolished the gulf between the centre and the periphery, between the official and the fringe – which is how a figure such as Bannon, a self-proclaimed 'Leninist' of the Right, can end up as Trump's chief strategist, with unrestricted access to the President, and a man like Jones, who rants about 'interdimensional travel' and insists that Obama 'is al-Qaeda', apparently has the ear of the Commander-in-Chief.[3]

These networks are also the ideal vector for conspiracy theories. In 2013, polls conducted by Fairleigh Dickinson University found that 63 per cent of registered American voters believed at least one such extraordinary claim (56 per cent of Democrats and 75 per cent of Republicans).[4] The following year, Eric Oliver and

Thomas Wood of the University of Chicago published research based on eight national surveys, conducted annually from 2006. They found that, in any given year, about 50 per cent of the public subscribed to at least one conspiracy theory. Among the most significant were: the 'Birther' claim that Barack Obama had not been born in Hawaii, but Kenya; the 'Truther' theory that the US government was involved in the 9/11 attacks; and the belief that the US Federal Reserve was behind the 2008 financial crisis.[5]

Some see an unexpected civic validity in the spread of myths. According to Sam Smith, writing in the *Progressive Review* in 1995, 'The poet understands that a myth is not a lie but the soul's version of the truth. One of the reasons so many stories are mangled by the media these days is because journalists have become unable to deal with the non-literal.'[6]

Maybe so: but, in the Post-Truth era, there is good reason to defend literalism. In his excellent study of conspiracy theories, the *Times* journalist David Aaronovitch suggests that the prevalence of such beliefs reflects a fundamental human yearning for narrative: 'we need story and may even be programmed to create it.' In this respect, 'The paradox is that … conspiracy theories are actually reassuring. They suggest that there is an explanation, that human agencies are powerful and that there is order rather than chaos. This makes redemption possible.' They are, Aaronovitch argues, a visceral protest against indifference – though none the less harmful for that.[7]

They also chime perilously with the priority accorded to emotion over evidence in the Post-Truth world. As Rob Brotherton notes in his study of these theories, 'We build a fortress of positive information around our beliefs, and we rarely step outside – or even peek out the window.'[8] In our assessment of such claims, however outlandish, we apply what psychologists call a 'positive test strategy' – looking for what we expect to find.

This inclination is buttressed by 'biased assimilation': we assess ambiguity in the light of our existing convictions. If we are inclined to think that governments behave with pathological secrecy, often in collaboration with lawbreakers, we will tend to reject the idea that Lee Harvey Oswald was the lone assassin of John F. Kennedy. If we suspect that all corporations are inherently wicked, we will heed claims – made on whatever basis – that genetically modified crops are dangerous.

The most profound such predisposition is religious belief. So when religion clashes with science, faith often prevails. As the findings of evolutionary research grow ever more exciting, creationism simply entrenches itself. It is remarkable to reflect that at least one in three Americans still reject Darwinian science and believe that the world was created a few thousand years ago. In 2005, the American Museum of Natural

History mounted an exhibition in honour of Darwin – but, exceptionally, was unable to secure sponsorship from corporations, apparently fearful of a creationist boycott. In 2007, a $27 million Creation Museum was opened in Petersburg, Kentucky, offering bumper stickers that declared: 'We're Taking Dinosaurs Back'. Just as the Brexiteers would urge UK voters, nine years later, to 'Take Back Control', so the creationists announced that they were reclaiming velociraptors for Christianity.

It was widely assumed in the first heady days of Web 2.0 that the digital revolution would spawn a global auto-correct facility; that falsehood would be driven out by the defence mechanism of e-accountability. Instead, it has sometimes seemed that the Internet is governed by an epistemological version of Gresham's Law: namely that bad money drives out good.

At the very least, the virus of falsehood has proved alarmingly resistant to treatment. Indeed, the treatment has often strengthened the disease. According to Brendan Nyhan, a political scientist at Dartmouth College, presenting someone who believes in a conspiracy theory with evidence that it is unfounded can often reinforce his or her belief: the so-called 'backfire effect'.[9]

We saw in the last chapter how robust the bogus idea of 'death panels' remained, quite immune to the justified objection that it has absolutely no basis in fact. An even more egregious example was the public response to the 'Birther' controversy – a furore first whipped up by supporters of Hillary Clinton in the 2008 Democratic presidential primaries, and very publicly exploited by Donald Trump as a pilot exercise for his own eventual candidacy.

Obama's initial response to the claim that, as a person of foreign birth, he was not qualified to run for the presidency, was to post an image of his short-form birth certificate. In July 2009, the director of Hawaii's Department of Health confirmed that the President's full birth records were indeed on file. Finally, in April 2011, he published his *long-form* birth certificate on the White House website. Case closed? Not a bit of it.

Before the publication of this definitive evidence, 45 per cent of US citizens admitted to doubts about Obama's birthplace. After the full certificate was posted, this figure fell – but only to 33 per cent. Then, in a startling rejection of the facts, the number began to *climb* again, reaching 41 per cent in January 2012. Like an infection resisting antibiotics, a virulent conspiracy theory can fend off even incontestable facts. Its popular strength depends not upon evidence, but upon *feeling* – the essence of Post-Truth culture. As the psychiatrist Karl Menninger put it: 'Attitudes are more important than facts.'

In separate research, brain imaging has revealed the neurological basis of this effect:

if we initially get a feeling of reward from an idea,
we will seek to replicate the feeling multiple times.
Each time, the reward center in the brain, the ventral
striatum and more specifically the nucleus accumbens
located within it, is triggered, and eventually other
parts of the instinctive brain learn to solidify the idea
into a fixed one. If we try to change our minds, a fear
center in the brain like the anterior insula warns us
that the danger is imminent. The powerful dorsolateral
prefrontal cortex can override these more primitive
brain centers and assert reason and logic, but it is slow
to act and requires a great deal of determination and
effort to do so. Hence, it is fundamentally unnatural
and uncomfortable to change our minds, and this is
reflected in the way our brains work.[10]

Thus, what looks like wilful resistance to the evidence
is often no more or less than the operations of biology.
Our brains countermand what we consider to be the
rational operations of our minds.

In the past, it was also commonplace to associate
conspiracy theories with the ignorance of the ill-
educated and the bigotry of rednecks. But this assumption was quite misplaced. According to recent research,
it is those who are most knowledgeable about politics
and science that tend to take extreme positions on,
for instance, climate change and death panels. Higher
education offers no real insulation against magical

thinking. As Brotherton puts it: 'Our beliefs come first; we make up reasons for them as we go along. Being smarter or having access to more information doesn't necessarily make us less susceptible to faulty beliefs.'[11]

WHO NEEDS SCIENCE?

These Post-Truth priorities have driven the rise of 'scientific denialism': the growing conviction that scientists, in league with government and pharmaceutical corporations ('Big Pharma'), are at war with nature and the best interests of humanity.[12] For some, the necessary response amounts to nothing more than eating organic food, buying local produce and taking large doses of vitamins and supplements every morning – hardly objectionable behaviour, whatever its merits. But the recoil from science becomes dangerous when it threatens public health, or the safety of others.

There is no better example of this than the sustained modern campaign against vaccination. This egregious form of denialism – a case study in Post-Truth – was triggered by a single study, published in the *Lancet* in 1998. On the basis of its findings, Dr Andrew Wakefield, one of the report's authors, told a press conference that there was a potential link between the measles, mumps and rubella vaccine, introduced in the UK ten years previously, and the rising incidence of diagnosed autism. I can well recall my own anxiety as a new parent, fretting over the alleged risk of the MMR.

As the claims gained currency in the media, uptake rates fell dramatically throughout the country, from 92 per cent to 73 per cent (and close to 50 per cent in parts of London), resulting in outbreaks of measles and fatalities. By June 2008, the disease had once more become endemic in Britain – fourteen years after its near-eradication.

As the press investigated the original study in more detail, Wakefield's methods were found to be wanting and conflicts of interest revealed. The paper was eventually retracted, ten of the thirteen authors withdrew their contributions and Wakefield's licence to practise medicine was withdrawn. But the verification process that had discredited him was weaker than the virus of fear he had injected into the popular bloodstream.

In 2001, Marie McCormick, professor of paediatrics at the Harvard School of Public Health, was asked to head the Immunization Safety Review Committee established by the Institute of Medicine (IOM). Though McCormick was not a specialist in the science of vaccination, this proved no impediment to her appointment. Indeed, it was the reason why she had been selected. As Anthony S. Fauci, the head of the National Institute of Allergy and Infectious Diseases, explained: 'Politically, there is simply no other way to do it. Experts are often considered tainted. It is an extremely frustrating fact of modern scientific life.'[13] This attitude to expertise, as we have seen, was to bleed into the political world and play a significant role in the Brexit referendum.

McCormick's committee delivered its report, *Vaccines and Autism*, in 2004, establishing beyond any reasonable doubt that there was no link between the two. Crucially, the committee found that unvaccinated children developed autism at the same or a higher rate than those who had been vaccinated. But the report was no match for the hysteria that had now consumed the public debate. The committee was forced to take extraordinary security measures during its final public meeting, after its members were subjected to plausible threats of violence, and even advised to keep the location of their hotel accommodation secret.

By this stage, the controversial mercury-based preservative Thimerosal had also been removed from vaccines – a step taken to reassure panicking parents but not mandated by scientific research. If anything, the measure *compounded* public anxiety, encouraging conspiracy theorists who believed that Thimerosal had been dangerous all along, that the science–pharmaceutical complex had known this but kept it secret, and that, as a result, there might be any number of other reasons to fear vaccinations. Meanwhile, the removal of the preservative did nothing to stop the rise in autism diagnosis.

What followed was an early parable in Post-Truth. It was beyond rational dispute that, in the developed world at least, vaccination had wiped out cholera, yellow fever, diphtheria, polio, smallpox and (pre-Wakefield) measles. But scientific evidence proved no match for the charisma of celebrity. In 2007, the model and television personality Jenny McCarthy, whose son Evan is autistic, appeared on Oprah Winfrey's show to take a stand on vaccination. Against the full might of the scientific establishment, she pitted her 'mommy instinct'. Challenged to produce her own evidence, she said: 'My science is named Evan, and he's at home. That's my science.' In the course of the controversy, doctors had often complained that the web had digitally turbo-charged false science. McCarthy turned this allegation on its head. 'The University of Google is where I got my degree from,' she declared.

The power of charismatic leadership to derail science is a familiar phenomenon. Thabo Mbeki, the former President of South Africa, gave immense emotional force to the bogus claim that HIV does not cause AIDS – and to the appalling epidemic in his country that remains a crisis to this day.

To the anti-vaccine crusade, Robert F. Kennedy Jr also brought the tinsel of political glamour. The IOM's report, he said, had sought 'to whitewash the risks of Thimerosal'. This was not true, but the charge, made by a Kennedy, had an undoubted impact. It is perhaps no surprise that President-elect Trump was drawn to Kennedy's claims, holding two conversations with him in January 2017 before his inauguration. At the time of writing, Kennedy still believes he is to head a new official committee on vaccine safety. But he has already got what he was after: the presidential seal of approval stamped upon his pseudo-science.[14]

Wakefield, meanwhile, has grasped that, in the strange alchemy of our times, academic infamy can be the basis for a celebrity of sorts: a means of relaunching his campaign and career. In April 2016, his movie *Vaxxed: From Cover-up to Catastrophe*, though withdrawn from the Tribeca Film Festival, was shown in Manhattan for the first time amid much hoopla and controversy.[15] Drenched in often clumsy appeals to emotion, the film hinged on the story of the so-called 'CDC whistleblower', Dr William Thompson, a scientist at the US Centers for Disease Control and Prevention.

Thompson, as the film relates, fed Brian Hooker, a biochemical engineer and father of an autistic son, with reams of data that Hooker – who had no training in epidemiology – subjected to his own personal analysis. His findings were published in an obscure journal in 2014, but rapidly whipped up an online storm.

Hooker claimed that the CDC had known all along that there was a link between MMR and autism, especially among African American males, but had concealed this information. Not surprisingly, this allegation generated widespread anxiety and anger, not least among African Americans and the parents of autistic children. But it had absolutely no basis in fact.

In his report, Hooker had committed elementary statistical errors, confusing a 'cohort study' (which follows people who do not have the disease in question and then traces what factors appear to increase the risk of contraction) with a 'case-control study' (in which two matched groups, one with the condition and one without, are compared to see what risk factors might account for the differences). In epidemiology, this is like saying an apple is a pear. Furthermore, the number of African American boys upon which he based his inflammatory conclusion was scandalously small.

In due course, Hooker's report was retracted by the journal that had published it. But *Vaxxed* simply repeats the allegations, presenting Hooker as the David who took on the Goliath of the health industry, and Wakefield as the oracular prophet vindicated. There is creative re-editing of Thompson's statements to strengthen the film's (spurious) case. The central claim of a cover-up by the CDC is simply not supported by the evidence. Stephanie Seneff, a computer scientist at MIT (again, not an epidemiologist), claims on camera that, by 2032, 80 per cent of boys will be autistic. The film is a farcical assault on medical science, unashamedly manipulative and unforgivably alarmist. But it has put Wakefield back on the front page of national newspapers.[16]

When truth falls in social value, the continuities in social practice it has supported are put in danger. Before the anti-vaccination movement arose, the diseases against which children were routinely inoculated were widely assumed to be a thing of the past. But, in public health as in politics, Post-Truth breeds astonishing volatility. When evidence-based research is trusted less than anecdotage, and institutional authority is heeded less than conspiracy theories, the consequences can be sudden and deadly. To be effective, vaccination depends upon 'herd immunity': that is, a level of uptake so high that the illness ceases to spread. Whether that immunity will survive the continuing hysteria over vaccination is an open question.[17]

ANTI-SEMITISM AND HOLOCAUST DENIAL IN THE DIGITAL AGE

No conspiracy theory in history has been more virulent or more catastrophic in its human cost than anti-Semitism. It is the most ancient hatred, but one that has constantly adapted and taken on newly malevolent forms. Hatred of Jews has always been found at both poles of the political spectrum. With grim predictability, the rise of populist nationalism and the alt-Right has coincided with a shocking increase in anti-Semitic incidents around the world. During the first month of 2017, forty-eight bomb threats were called in to Jewish community centres across America. From August 2015 to July 2016, the Anti-Defamation League identified 2.6 million tweets that included language hostile to Jews. In Germany, the number of anti-Semitic incidents rose from 194 between January and September 2015 to 461 during the same period in 2016. In the UK, anti-Semitic hate crimes rose to record levels in 2016, according to the Community Security Trust, which recorded 1,309 such incidents during the year, a 36 per cent increase on the 2015 total.

No less alarming is the reinvigoration of Holocaust denial, especially online. At the time of writing, if you enter the words 'Was the Holocaust real?' into the Google search engine, the first page of results includes the headlines: 'Holocaust Against Jews is a Total Lie – Proof'; 'Is the Holocaust a Hoax?'; 'Was there really a Holocaust?'; 'THE HOLOCAUST AND THE FOUR MILLION VARIANT'; 'How the "Holocaust" was faked'; and 'Jewish Scholar Refutes The Holocaust'. There could scarcely be a more brutal reminder that algorithms, in their current form, are indifferent to veracity.

In one sense, modern anti-Semitism is the template for what has become Post-Truth. Its founding charter, an essential source for Hitler when he was writing *Mein Kampf*, is the document known as *The Protocols of the Learned Elders of Zion.* Supposedly the minutes of a secret gathering of the supreme council of Jews, the text consists of twenty-four brief sermons alleged to have been delivered by the Chief Elder, and was first published in 1903 in the Russian newspaper *Znamia*. After the Russian Revolution and the First World War, its influence was felt around the world, feeding the myth that a cartel of Jewish financiers was responsible for the Great Depression.

'The only statement I care to make about the *Protocols*,' said the notorious anti-Semite Henry Ford, 'is that they fit in with what is going on.' One could hardly ask for a more pointed instance of confirmation bias, or of the unashamed primacy of visceral feeling over empirical reality.[18] What did it matter to a bigot like Ford that the *Protocols* were demonstrably, conclusively, a feeble forgery?

This had been quite clear since 1920 when a German scholar, Joseph Stanjek, traced the similarities between the much-circulated document and a work of fiction, *Biarritz* (1868), written by another German, Hermann Goedsche, under the nom de plume Sir John Retcliffe. Much of the material in the *Protocols* was plagiarised from another work of fiction, written by a Frenchman named Maurice Joly, describing an imagined dialogue between Machiavelli and Montesquieu in the underworld. In time, it would be established beyond question that the texts had been artlessly spliced together by the

Okhrana, the Russian secret police. But the absolute inauthenticity of the *Protocols* had been demonstrated well before the rise of Hitler.

This did not trouble the Nazi leader in the slightest. Like Ford, he regarded the document as real because it chimed with his own illimitable hatred for the Jews. As he wrote in *Mein Kampf,* 'the best criticism applied to [the *Protocols*] is reality. He who examines the historical development of the past hundred years, from the points of view of this book, will also immediately understand the clamour of the Jewish press.'[19] If ideas have a genealogy, this was a germinal moment for the trends that have coalesced, almost a century later, in the Post-Truth era.

The same disregard for evidence underpins Holocaust denial. Though many have been associated with this vile phenomenon, no one has rivalled the prominence of David Irving, the prolific historian and idol of the far Right. In 2000, Irving sued the American academic Deborah Lipstadt and her publisher, Penguin Books, in the High Court over her description of him in the book *Denying the Holocaust*:

Irving is one of the most dangerous spokespersons for Holocaust denial. Familiar with historical evidence, he bends it until it conforms with his ideological leanings and political agenda. A man who is convinced that Britain's great decline was accelerated by its decision to go to war with Germany, he is most facile at taking accurate information and shaping it to confirm his conclusions. A review of his recent book, *Churchill's War*, which appeared in *New York Review of Books*, accurately analyzed his practice of applying a double standard to evidence. He demands 'absolute documentary proof' when it comes to proving the Germans guilty, but he relies on highly circumstantial evidence to condemn the Allies. This is an accurate description not only of Irving's tactics, but of those of deniers in general.[20]

For Irving, this was an attack upon his academic credentials, as well as an accusation that he denied the reality of the Shoah. Under the English law of libel, the burden of proof lay with Lipstadt, the defendant. She knew that much more than her intellectual reputation was at stake. Otiose as it might seem to anyone with a shred of regard for history and the power of evidence, her legal team was obliged to demonstrate that Irving was wrong about the Holocaust; that there had been gas chambers at Auschwitz, that the deaths at the camps were overwhelmingly the consequence of genocide rather than disease; and that the euphemistic language often used by Nazis to describe the industrialised slaughter ('resettlement') did not have any bearing upon its literal truth.

Should Irving prevail in the trial, Lipstadt grasped, the deniers would have won a famous victory, and the reality of the greatest crime every committed would be questioned with exponentially increased confidence. In her account of the case – later turned into a film, *Denial,* starring Timothy Spall and Rachel Weisz – she recalled the sense of responsibility to the victims and survivors of the Holocaust she felt on the night before she learned of the verdict:

> Around 11 P.M., Ben Meed, president of the American Gathering of Jewish Holocaust Survivors and a survivor of the Warsaw Ghetto, called. A compact white-haired man, Ben's life was the world of Holocaust survivors. 'Deborah,' he said, 'tonight you can sleep soundly because none of us will be sleeping.' He did not have to identify the 'us'. There is a Jewish aphorism: 'Things which come from the heart enter the heart.' And so it was … I imagined myself surrounded by a band of resolute angels, whose lives had been shaped by the Holocaust and its attendant horrors.[21]

The following day, Lipstadt learned that Irving had been categorically defeated. In his 355-page ruling, Judge Gray said that he had 'significantly misrepresented what the evidence, objectively examined, reveals'. His 'falsification of the historical record was deliberate and … motivated by a desire to present events in a manner consistent with his own ideological beliefs even if that involved distortion and manipulation of historical evidence'. Irving 'was misrepresenting the historical evidence when he told audiences in Australia, Canada, and the US ... that the shooting of the Jews in the east was arbitrary, unauthorized, and undertaken by individual groups or commanders'. The judge declared it 'incontrovertible that Irving qualifies as a Holocaust denier'. He had often denied the existence of the gas chambers at Auschwitz and 'in the most offensive terms'.[22]

The Lipstadt trial was rightly perceived as a landmark victory in the struggle against denial, the forensic debunking of a monstrous insult to six million dead. But it did not mark the end of the struggle so much as the beginning of a new phase of battle. Holocaust denial had been definitively driven from the realm of academic history: no serious scholar, whatever their ideological beliefs, would want to court the global humiliation visited upon Irving in the High Court.

But falsehood is cunning, adapting to suit new circumstances and metastasising however it can. A poll in 2014 of more than 53,000 people in over 100 countries showed that only a third of the world's population believed that the Holocaust had been accurately recorded in historical accounts. Thirty per cent said it was probably true that 'Jews still talk too much about what happened to them in the Holocaust'. In a worrying portent for the future, those under sixty-five were much more likely to say that they thought the facts about the genocide had been distorted – including, among respondents under that age, 22 per cent of Christians, 51 per cent of Muslims and 28 per cent of those with no declared religion.[23]

This generational difference has been compounded by the resurgence of anti-Semitism and the buzz of digital doubt. A study by Scott Darnell, of the Harvard Kennedy School of Government, published in 2010, concluded that 'knowledge of the Holocaust is relatively low in the U.S., and that, over the past decade, the number and concentration of organized anti-semitic hate groups has risen (especially in the South and Mountain West)'. Though Darnell detected a decline in the overall number of anti-Semitic incidents – a pattern that was reversed in subsequent years – he also found that states

with a larger and more concentrated Jewish population tend to experience more antisemitic incidents, while organized hate group activity is most heavily concentrated in states with the smallest and least concentrated Jewish population; foreign-born Hispanics, African Americans, and those with low levels of education are particularly prone to harboring antisemitic beliefs. There is strong evidence to suggest that Holocaust denial has garnered an increasing amount of U.S. media coverage over the past decade and continues to grow in prevalence on the Internet.[24]

As depressing as this is, it should not surprise us. In the Post-Truth era, even the most erudite turn, by reflex, to the Internet as their first port of call when seeking instant information. Many never get beyond what Jenny McCarthy christened the 'University of Google' when conducting their enquiries. And, as we have seen, those who enter a question about the Holocaust into a search engine will not be rewarded with the learning of great scholars such as Martin Gilbert, Nikolaus Wachsmann or Laurence Rees, or the eyewitness accounts of Primo Levi, Viktor Frankl or Elie Wiesel. Their digital dividend will be a mixed bag of summary pages and outright garbage about the 'Holo-hoax' as a conspiracy of 'Hollywood-style Jewry' and the 'Biggest Lie'. Ludicrous as these sites are, they represent an incoming tide of unfiltered venom that we dare not ignore. When healthy pluralism is supplanted by unhealthy relativism, the cultural assumption is that all opinions are equally valid. Where are the forces urging the young to exercise their critical faculties when they stare at their smartphones?

As Hofstadter knew, conspiracy theories have always been deployed as an explanatory device. In the Post-Truth era, as we have seen, they have proliferated dramatically, as their intrinsic appeal to the human mind has been enhanced by a range of pressures and transformations. In the twenty-first century, the conspiracist mentality is partly a response to a world of sometimes bewildering change – globalisation and its discontents, unprecedented population mobility, the digital revolution, rapidly mutating forms of extremism and terrorism, the breathtaking possibilities of biotechnology.

Those who have drilled down into this new stratum of human history discover structural challenges that have hardly been acknowledged, much less answered. Martin Ford's *The Rise of the Robots* describes a world in which education, still desirable as a promoter of civic decency, will not be able to keep pace with job-destroying automation – forcing the state to pay all citizens a basic income.[25]

Yuval Noah Harari's remarkable book *Homo Deus* pursues the argument further, foretelling the supplanting of professional as well as semi-skilled labour by 'highly intelligent algorithms'. Especially unnerving is Harari's prophecy that mankind will divide into 'an algorithmic upper class owning most of our planet' and 'a new massive class: people devoid of any economic, political or even artistic value'.[26]

But you do not have to read such texts to sense that dramatic upheaval in the way we live and work is at hand. That much is clear from the declining number of tellers in banks, from the replacement of shops by online delivery and in reports that Amazon is considering a new kind of supermarket that will require only three staff members.[27]

In this setting, it is scarcely surprising that, as we have seen, the idea of 'control' is so appealing. Conspiracy theories, to quote one academic psychologist, 'pave over messy, bewildering, ambiguous reality with a simple explanation'.[28] They offer a matrix of order, whose appealing simplicity eclipses its absurdities. As Dr Wilbur Larch observes in John Irving's *The Cider House Rules*, falsehood can be a means of reclaiming power:

> When you lie, it makes you feel in charge of your life.
> Telling lies is very seductive to orphans. I know … I
> know because I tell them, too. I love to lie. When you
> lie, you feel as if you have cheated fate – your own, and
> everybody else's.[29]

For the parents of autistic children, the claim that vaccination is the culprit – however often debunked – offers the partial comfort of causality and culpability, emotionally preferable to the idea that the universe is cruel and arbitrary. For those who do not trust conventional medicine – or the government – there is an inherent appeal in the theory that the 'chemtrails' supposedly left in the sky by aircraft cause illness or infertility. For many, the inherent silliness of this proposition is overshadowed by its internal coherence: it imposes a structure upon the discordant music of chance. In a world of relentless change and disruption, who is to say that the consolations of the conspiracist will be defeated by the cool rigours of truth?

4

THE CRASH OF THE PHILOSOPHER'S STONE: POST-MODERNISM, IRONY AND THE POST-TRUTH ERA

THE POWER OF IDEAS

Among the most pernicious myths to afflict our times is the insistence that there is an unbridgeable gulf between an intellectual, 'over-educated' elite and 'ordinary people' in the 'real world'.[1] This claim, repeated ad nauseam in recent years, has been fundamental, though not confined, to the rhetoric of the populist Right. The old quip that certain people are 'too clever by half' is no longer made in jest. It is advanced as a wedge argument, to reinforce the bogus notion of a 'metropolitan class' acting against the best interests of the majority, promoting ideas of no relevance to the great mass of the public.

Not only is this argument divisive and patronising (as though those outside great cities were incapable of cerebration), it also ignores the overwhelming evidence on our historical doorstep of the power of ideas. Reduced to its essentials, the twentieth century was a horrendously costly experiment in totalitarian ideology – Marxist and fascist – demonstrating beyond doubt the porousness between intellectual life and the world of action.

Had Marx not laboured over *Das Kapital* in the Reading Room of the British Museum, after his exile to London in 1849, the history of the last century might have been very different. To quote Isaiah Berlin's famous warning in *Two Concepts of Liberty*:

When ideas are neglected by those who ought to attend to them – that is to say, those who have been trained to think critically about ideas – they often acquire an unchecked momentum and an irresistible power over multitudes of men that may grow too violent to be affected by rational criticism. Over a hundred years ago, the German poet Heine warned the French not to underestimate the power of ideas: philosophical concepts nurtured in the stillness of a professor's study could destroy a civilization.[2]

No less than any other age, the Post-Truth era has its own intellectual geology – a basis in the post-modern philosophy of the late twentieth century, often abstruse and impenetrable, that has been popularised and distilled to the point that it is recognisable – albeit without attribution – in many features of contemporary culture. As esoteric as much of it may seem, it is worth persevering with this line of inquiry. It is impossible to fight Post-Truth without an understanding of its deepest roots.

POST-MODERNISM, GOOD AND BAD

Post-modernism is notoriously resistant to precise definition, to the point that some deny it has any coherence as a school of thought. It is certainly not a homogenous body of work and, as a consequence, has had a diffuse and even contradictory impact upon the world outside academia. Its principal protagonists (Michel Foucault, Jean-François Lyotard, Jacques Derrida, Jean Baudrillard and Richard Rorty, to name but five) retain a certain grip upon the contemporary intellectual imagination. Less certain is what, precisely, they meant, and what they have bequeathed to the world today.

For the purposes of this book, two aspects of post-modernist thinking are worth noting. On the credit side, it encouraged the idea that an increasingly pluralist society would need to acknowledge and heed multiple voices: the stories of gender, ethnic minorities, sexual orientation and cultural tradition. Post-modern thinkers such as Richard Ashley, Derrida and Foucault urged their readers to question and deconstruct language, visual idiom, institutions and received wisdom, and to ask how words, stories, art and architecture might enshrine forms of power and 'hegemony' to which we would otherwise remain blind. Though their jargon-ridden prose was often indigestible, it was part of a much broader yearning in the final quarter of the last century for inclusivity, diversity, personal liberty and civil rights. And this achievement stands.

At the same time, it would be naive to deny that the principal thinkers associated with this loose-knit school, by questioning the very notion of objective reality, did much to corrode the notion of truth. Their natural terrain was irony, surface, estrangement and fragmentation. Post-modern philosophers preferred to understand language and culture as 'social constructs', political phenomena that reflected the distribution of power across class, race, gender and sexuality, rather than the abstract ideals of classical philosophy. And if everything is a 'social construct', then who is to say what is false? What is to stop the purveyor of 'fake news' from claiming to be a digital desperado, fighting the wicked 'hegemony' of the mainstream media?

From the start, the opponents of post-modernism objected that it was no more than a flashy repackaging of an ancient argument between believers in truth and relativists. In the fifth century BC, the Thracian philosopher Protagoras had argued that 'man is the measure of all things' and that anything 'is to me such as it appears to me, and is to you such as it appears to you'. Nietzsche had gone much further, insisting that human nature was positively *hostile* to the notion of truth:

> In man this art of simulation reaches its peak ... the constant fluttering around the single flame of vanity is so much the rule and the law that almost nothing is more incomprehensible than how an honest and pure urge for truth could have arisen among men. They are deeply immersed in illusions and dream images; their eye glides only over the surface of things and sees 'forms'; their feeling nowhere leads into truth, but contents itself with the reception of stimuli, playing, as it were, a game of blind man's buff on the backs of things.[3]

The great American psychologist and philosopher William James made a similar point in less excitable language:

> Reality 'independent' of human thinking is a thing very hard to find. It reduces to the notion of what is just entering into experience and yet to be named, or else to some imagined aboriginal presence in experience,

before any belief about the presence had arisen, before
any human conception had been applied. It is what is
absolutely dumb and evanescent, the mere ideal limit
of our minds ... If so vulgar an expression were allowed
us, we might say that wherever we find it, it has already
been *faked*.[4]

In other words: the subversion of truth as an attainable ideal is as old as philosophy itself. What the 'po-mo' theorists did was to present a new kind of relativism, fit for, and inspired by, its times. In his book *The Postmodern Condition*, first published in 1979, the French philosopher Jean-François Lyotard proposed 'an incredulity towards meta-narratives' – the 'grand narratives' that had underpinned philosophy since the Enlightenment – and the very idea of 'truth-value'.[5]

In a later work, *The Inhuman* (1988), he posed, prophetically, 'the questions born of the spectacular introduction of what are called the new technologies into the production, diffusion, distribution and consumption of cultural commodities. Why mention the fact here? Because they are in the process of transforming culture into an industry.'[6]

Lyotard regarded the twentieth-century revolution in science – quantum physics, for a start – as profoundly significant to philosophers: 'The problems out of which emerged non-Euclidian geometry, axiomatic forms of arithmetic and non-Newtonian physics are also those which gave rise to the theories of communication and information.'[7]

His conclusion was dispiriting to the point of hopelessness: 'Let us at least bear witness, and again, and for no-one, to thinking as disaster, nomadism, difference and redundancy. Let's write our graffiti since we can't engrave ... The witness is a traitor.'[8] All of this was doubtless stimulating in the seminar room and the cafés of the *Rive Gauche*, but as a practical template for living it was a counsel of despair.

To take another example: Baudrillard was drawn to the science of signs, or semiotics. In his best-known work, *Simulacra and Simulation* (1981), he argued:

> We live in a world where there is more and more information, and less and less meaning ... Despite efforts to reinject message and content, meaning is lost and devoured faster than it can be reinjected ... Everywhere socialization is measured by the exposure to media messages. Whoever is underexposed to the media is desocialized or virtually asocial ... where we think that information produces meaning, the opposite occurs.[9]

Communications technology, in other words, would subvert our inherited notions of the real. Bear in mind that Baudrillard's prophecy of social media becoming both a measure of belonging and a source of disinformation – 'fake news' – was made eight years before

Sir Tim Berners-Lee invented the World Wide Web, twenty-three before the launch of Facebook and twenty-five before the creation of Twitter. In this, as in other respects, post-modernist texts paved the way for Post-Truth.[10]

RUST ON THE METAL OF TRUTH
– AND ITS CONSEQUENCES

Reduced to its ideological essentials, post-modernism was a theoretical campaign that appealed to the disenchanted Left, longing to make sense of a century in which the old certainties of the Marxist avant-garde had crumbled before them. Often incomprehensible in its terminology and intellectual skittishness, its chief protagonists scrambled to find a new politics of social emancipation amid the wreckage. As noted above, they did not entirely fail.

Yet they did not entirely succeed either. Released into the ether of campuses, the media and cultural life, post-modernism became less of a coherent philosophy and more of a *mood*. It gave intellectual prestige to fashionable cynicism and a fresh face to relativism.[11] Whatever the intentions of its founders – which were often opaque – it became a rust on the metal of truth.

This did not matter as long as there was a fuzzy consensus that truth was still a priority. But, as we have seen, that consensus has collapsed. Since Trump has declared that he has no time to read, one can be certain that he is unacquainted with Baudrillard or Lyotard. Whatever else he is, the forty fifth President is no post-modernist. Indeed, his closest adviser, Stephen Bannon, is openly dedicated to the restoration of the old conservative, Christian hegemony – precisely what the post-modernists sought to deconstruct.

Trump is the unlikely *beneficiary* of a philosophy that he has probably never heard of and would certainly despise. His rise to the most powerful office in the world, unhindered by care for the truth, accelerated by the awesome force of social media, was, in its way, the ultimate post-modern moment.

At a 2015 campaign rally in Birmingham, Alabama, he declared: 'I watched when the World Trade Center came tumbling down. And I watched in Jersey City … where thousands and thousands of people were cheering as that building was coming down. Thousands of people were cheering.' This was a complete falsehood.[12] But Trump simply refused to acknowledge his mendacity. 'I have a very good memory, I'll tell you,' he said when challenged on NBC. 'I saw it somewhere on television many years ago. And I never forgot it.'[13]

Baudrillard and his peers could not have conjured up a better example of 'hyper-reality' – the mode of discourse in which the gap between the real and the imaginary disappears. Trump had confected a hyper-real recollection, and would not retract his claim simply because pedants could find no evidence to support it. It is an arresting reflection that, etched into the long, Parisian paragraphs of convoluted, post-modern prose, so often dismissed as indulgent nonsense, was a bleak omen of the political future.

Post-truth represents surrender to this analysis: a recognition by the producers and consumers of information that reality is now so elusive and our perspectives as individuals and groups so divergent that it is no longer meaningful to speak of, or seek, the truth. Pluralists have long spoken of 'incommensurable values'. The epistemology of Post-Truth urges us to accept that there are 'incommensurable realities' and that prudent conduct consists in choosing sides rather than evaluating evidence.

This no more than the post-modern idea of 'community agreement' – or, as Richard Rorty has put it: 'Truth is what my colleagues will let me get away with.'[14] It obliterates the notion of objective reality and replaces it with prevailing wisdom, folklore and the pixelated images we see on screen.

This is perfectly predicted in *Wag the Dog*, Barry Levinson's movie satire of 1997, which describes the 'pageant' of a fictional war invented to distract voters' attention from a presidential scx scandal. The political fixer, Conrad Brean (Robert De Niro), approaches a Hollywood mogul, Stanley Motss (Dustin Hoffman), to 'produce' the military 'pageant' of an imaginary conflict with Albania:

Conrad: You watched the Gulf War – what do you see day after day? The one smart bomb falling down the chimney. The truth? I was in the building when we shot that shot – we shot in a studio, Falls Church, Virginia. One-tenth scale model of a building.

Stanley: Is that true?

Conrad: How the fuck do we know? You take my point?

Later in the story, Conrad is dismayed when the CIA conspires with the President's electoral opponent to declare the non-existent war at an end. But the producer is not so easily dissuaded, insisting that it is his picture and nobody else's. Conrad counters that the television news is reporting that the war is over and that is what counts. What the two men are arguing about is not reality, but a competition between two fictions. They are talking about Post-Truth.

Again, remember the power of ideas: their osmotic effect upon the world of deeds as well as thoughts. And it is hard to overstate the potential cost of this particular cultural trend. In his 'Bill for the More General Diffusion of Knowledge' (1779), Thomas Jefferson expressed pithily the necessity of truth as a bulwark against authoritarianism and dictatorship:

> Even under the best forms [of government], those entrusted with power have, in time, and by slow operations, perverted it into tyranny; and it is believed that the most effectual means of preventing this would be, to illuminate, as far as practicable, the minds of the people at large, and more especially to give them knowledge of those facts, which history exhibiteth, that ... they may be enabled to know ambition under all its shapes, and prompt to exert their natural powers to defeat its purposes.[15]

The salient feature of Jefferson's proposal was its *practical* nature. He understood the social necessity of truth, as well as its philosophical significance. Likewise, Kant's obsession with the truth would doubtless be scorned by some today as 'virtue-signalling'. But he was right to anticipate the viral consequences of indifference to falsehood: 'For a lie always harms another; if not some other particular man, still it harms mankind generally, for it vitiates the source of law itself.'[16]

Sir Francis Bacon's inductive method – proceeding from observation to generalisations sustained only by the facts established – was the basis of the scientific revolution, and all it has yielded. In her masterly history of the modern fact – 'the epistemological unit that organizes most of the knowledge projects of the past four centuries' – Professor Mary Poovey of New York University shows that commercial practice was also essential to the increasing value assigned to verifiable information. She particularly identifies two institutions of early mercantile capitalism: double-entry bookkeeping and the informal systems of agreement between merchants.[17]

In other words: the rise of truth as a binding force in scientific, legal, political and commercial practice was a gradual and hard-won achievement. It is a single currency, furthermore, whose value is determined by the extent to which it is defended in each of these interconnected spheres. Those who blithely assume that its threatened collapse in the political world will have no ramifications in the rest of civic society are in for a shock. The heedless marshalling of information – my 'fake news' versus yours – imperils the value of evidence wherever it is deployed. There is a twitching thread that connects the lies of Trump to the pseudo-science of anti-vaccine campaigners. The question is how we react, what we do next.

REASONS TO BE CHEERFUL

I do not think our intellectual immunity is shot: not yet, anyway. It is heartening, for instance, that Orwell's *Nineteen Eighty-Four* rose to the top of Amazon's charts days after Kellyanne Conway urged Americans to embrace 'alternative facts'.[18] The classic novel describes a totalitarian world, rather than a fragmented, globalised, inter-connected and hyper-mobile society such as our own. Orwell did not anticipate the transformative power of technology, imagining instead that the new power blocs would strictly control its advance to maintain the deprivation and lack of comfort that was essential to their control of the masses. But the symmetries between his fiction and our experience are clear enough. The idea of 'doublethink' – 'the power of holding two contradictory beliefs in one's mind, and accepting both of them' – is the direct ancestor of Post-Truth.

So, too, is the warning issued to Winston Smith by his Inner Party interrogator, O'Brien, that 'reality is not external. Reality exists in the human mind, and nowhere else … Whatever the Party holds to be truth, *is* truth. It is impossible to see reality except by looking through the eyes of the Party.' In response to Winston's maxim that 'Freedom is the freedom to say that two plus two make four', O'Brien tortures him until he sees not four but 'a forest of fingers … moving in a sort of dance, weaving in and out, disappearing behind one another and reappearing again'. He disputes Winston's objection that 'You don't even control the climate or the law of gravity. And there are disease, pain, death—'

O'Brien silenced him by a movement of his hand. 'We control matter because we control the mind. Reality is inside the skull … There is nothing that we could not do. Invisibility, levitation – anything. I could float off this floor like a soap bubble if I wish to … You must get rid of those nineteenth-century ideas about the laws of Nature. We make the laws of Nature.'[19]

It is encouraging that some, at least, are turning once more to Orwell's novel, or to Sinclair Lewis's *It Can't Happen Here* (about the election of a fascist president), or to Hannah Arendt's classic analysis, *The Origins of Totalitarianism*.

Satire, too, offers grounds for hope. As a genre, it is most successful when it finds humour in contemporary anxiety. So it is reassuring to recall that the writers of *The Thick of It*, Armando Iannucci and Jesse Armstrong, captured the essence of Post-Truth in the very first episode of the programme's first season in 2005 – in which the terrifying spin doctor, Malcolm Tucker, is explaining to a besieged minister, Hugh Abbot, how to turn the tanker of a potentially damaging story:

Hugh: What, erm … What are we going to do now?

Malcolm: You're going to completely reverse your position.

Hugh: Look, no, hang on a second. Hang on, Malcolm. It's not actually that, erm – That's going to be quite hard, really.

Malcolm: Yes, well, the announcement that you didn't make today – you *did*.

Hugh: No, no, I didn't. And there were television cameras there while I was not doing it.

Malcolm: Fuck them.

Hugh: I'm not quite sure how … what level of reality I'm supposed to be operating on.

Malcolm: Look, this is what they run with. I tell them that you said it, they believe that you said it. They don't *really* believe you said it – they know that you never said it.

Hugh: Right.

Malcolm: But it's in their interests to say you said it – because if they don't, they're not going to get what you say tomorrow or the next day when I decide to tell them what it is you're saying.

Hugh: Yeah.

This exchange makes light of the systematic undermining of truth in which politicians and media collude. But it also reflects the capacity of the best satire to act as an early warning system. What Malcolm describes to Hugh is the pernicious contract that lies at the heart of Post-Truth. Their conversation is funny precisely because it addresses the subconscious anxiety of the audience about that contract. It sends up an intellectual flare.

If Post-Truth takes some of its inspiration from post-modern ideas, it is worth noting that those ideas have fallen dramatically out of intellectual favour in the past few decades. The late novelist and academic David Foster Wallace was among the first to make a public issue of their limitations. Though raised in what he and others called the 'po-mo' age, he questioned what he called 'institutionalised irony': not the healthy irony of satire, scepticism and well-targeted irreverence, the lifeblood of a democracy, but, as Wallace put it, the 'enfeebling variety', leading nowhere and achieving nothing. His choice of metaphor was telling: 'Third World rebels are great at exposing and overthrowing corrupt hypocritical regimes but they seem noticeably less great at the mundane, non-negative task of then establishing a superior governing alternative … make no mistake: irony tyrannizes us.'[20]

In place of post-modernism, a school of New Realism has arisen, notably in the work of the Italian philosopher

Maurizio Ferraris. Initially influenced by Lyotard, Foucault and (especially) Derrida, Ferraris later abandoned relativism and embraced a form of realistic objectivism. His previous commitment, he acknowledged, 'was politically insufficient, as it presented itself as a way to change the world for better, emancipating it, but in fact it was just a way to create mass illusions governed by power – as media populism has demonstrated. "There are no facts, but only interpretations" has ended up meaning "The reason of the strongest is always the best."' Realism could be observed in characteristics of 'resistance' (I cannot use a screwdriver to drink orange juice) and of 'affordance' (but I can use it to tighten a screw or make a hole).[21]

'The aim of philosophy,' he writes in *Positive Realism* (2014), 'is not to create an alternative world to that posited by science, whether through reference to commonsense and the "world of life" or through the transcendence of commonsense and the search for paradoxes. It is a matter of bridging the divide between science and commonsense, between what we think (or what scientists think) and what we experience.'[22]

This new optimism is also to be found in the writings of the celebrated philosopher, novelist and journalist Umberto Eco, who died in 2016. Three years before his death, he delivered a speech in Athens, mulling over the realism he had embraced in an earlier book: 'Remember that not even Nietzsche denied the existence of "terrible forces" that constantly press upon us. In my *Kant and the Platypus*, I called these terrible forces the hard core of Being.'

He continued:

In speaking of a hard core, I did not mean something like a stable kernel which we might identify sooner or later – not the Law of Laws, but, more prudently, lines of resistance that render some of our approaches fruitless. This idea of 'lines of resistance', by which something which does not depend on our interpretations challenges them, can represent a form of Minimal or Negative Realism according to which facts, if scarcely [they] tell me if I am right, frequently tell me that I am wrong.

Eco concluded: 'If so, Being may not be comparable to a one-way street, but to a network of multi-lane freeways along which one can travel in more than one direction; but despite this some roads will nonetheless remain dead-ends.'[23]

Why should we care about the rarefied musings of Ferraris and Eco? Because, as Isaiah Berlin said, ideas count. More often than we care to acknowledge, philosophers are cultural scouts, mapping out previously uncharted terrain upon which we will all soon be walking. If the post-modern thinkers were the inadvertent prophets of Post-Truth, it may be that the New Realists are pathfinders for a fresh surge in the value of evidence and accuracy.

As the philosopher Simon Blackburn has put it: 'We can take the post-modernist inverted commas off things that ought to matter to us: truth, reason, objectivity and confidence. They are no less, if no more, than the virtues that we should all cherish as we try to understand the bewildering world about us.'[24]

There is no certainty in such a renaissance, no historical inevitability. But it is a mistake to give in to the counsels of despair that followed Brexit and the election of Trump. Relativism succeeds only if we allow it to do so. As David Hume wrote, in a famous metaphor, the differences that are innate to a complex world need not be insuperable: 'The Rhine flows north, the Rhine south; yet both spring from the *same* mountain, and also are actuated in their opposite directions, by the *same* principle of gravity. The different inclinations of the ground, on which they run, cause all the difference of their courses.'[25]

In a multi-ethnic, multi-faith society, the objective can never be to enforce absolute uniformity: that would be ethically indefensible as well as appallingly tedious. It is to identify the core of cultural norms, legal duties and social responsibilities to which all citizens must sign up, whatever their private opinions.

Diversity is, and will continue to be, a given, whatever the new cohort of nativists claim to the contrary.

The challenge is to identify the common ground of social, intellectual and practical exchange upon which all agree. Post-Truth feeds upon alienation, dislocation and stultified silence. The greatest civic task that lies ahead is to empty the trough.

5

'THE STENCH OF LIES': STRATEGIES TO DEFEAT POST-TRUTH

NO TURNING BACK

The survival of civilisation, reason and scientific truth is not preordained. The roots of the Golden Age of Islam are usually detected in the reigns of the great Abbasid caliph Harun al-Rashid (786–809) and his foundation of the House of Wisdom in Baghdad. The achievements of this era were prodigious: in education, mathematics, natural science, the arts and philosophy (notably the great twelfth-century Aristotelian Ibn Rushd, or Averroes). Yet, symbolically at least, the Golden Age was brought to an end by the destruction of Baghdad and the House of

Wisdom in 1258 by the invading Mongol ruler Hulagu Khan.

In 1421, China was a global hub of scientific inquiry and learning, an expansionist society of seemingly limitless intellectual ambition and geographical horizon. Yet the newly constructed Forbidden City was struck by lightning on 9 May in that year: an omen that the emperor Zhu Di feared was a terrible warning from the gods that the Middle Kingdom, in its ambition, commerce and zeal for construction, had become irreligious. The consequences of this single meteorological event were momentous. In 1424, Zhu Di's son, Zhu Gaozhi, ordered the building, repair and voyages of treasure fleets to cease at once. Overseas trade was later forbidden, as, for a time, was the learning of foreign languages. Rejecting its achievements on the high seas and in science, China retreated into a long isolation.

Our own Post-Truth era is a taste of what happens when a society relaxes its defence of the values that underpin its cohesion, order and progress: the values of veracity, honesty and accountability. Those values are not self-preserving. Their maintenance is the product of human decision, agency and collaboration. There is no historical pendulum that means that Post-Truth will inevitably recede. Nor is its current prevalence the work of a lone individual. Those who believe that the problems discussed in these pages will pass when President Trump leaves office (20 January 2025, if he wins and completes a second term) are confusing the leaves of the weed with its roots. Running out the clock is not an option.

So what to do? Post-Truth is a tendency, and a deeply alarming one. But it is not a terminus. Those made despondent by this wrong turn need to get off their knees and fight back. The worst possible response is voiceless passivity. The best is to identify and champion those practical steps that will defend truth from its antagonists, enhance its value and ensure its centrality in a radically transformed social and technological context.

This is absolutely *not* a restorationist or heritage project, a mission to turn back the clock to an imagined past of untarnished veracity. There was never such a time and, even if there had been, it would be impossible to recreate. It is a central claim of this book that digital technology has been the principal infrastructure of Post-Truth. But it would be ludicrous – and profoundly anti-democratic – to recommend the rolling back of this revolution.[1] The question is what best to do within its rapidly shifting borders.

THE SCRUTINY SPECTRUM

Information overload means that we must all become editors: sifting, checking, assessing what we read. Just as children are taught how to understand printed texts, their critical faculties should be trained to meet the very different challenges of a digital feed. What Kitemarks, if any, recommend a particular post or site as a reliable source? Are the claims advanced supported by links, footnotes or credible data? The inclination of some teachers to treat the Internet as a second-rate resource misses the point. For the generation now at school, and those to come, it is the *only* significant resource.

As books themselves migrate to the cloud – a process already well advanced – those of us who still enjoy physical texts as artefacts of the mind will be regarded as antique-lovers. It should be a core task of primary – not secondary – education to teach children how to select and discriminate from the digital torrent.

Learning how to navigate the web with discernment is the most pressing cultural mission of our age. The best podcasts already lend assistance in this undertaking – helping the listener or viewer to reflect upon the digital outpourings of the week, or the day, and subject them to analysis (albeit of varying rigour). In its simplicity and directness, this new form of content – usually two talking heads debating a contemporary topic at length – is the punk descendant of the Socratic dialogue.

This is the soft end of the scrutiny spectrum. The open-source investigations of citizen-journalist groups such as Bellingcat – piecing together thousands of fragments of online data to reach their conclusions – will also contribute to a new system of checks and balances. Though still controversial, Bellingcat's high-tech investigations into the fate of Malaysian Airlines Flight 17 on 17 July 2014, sifting through huge quantities of digital information, have shown what can be done.[2]

In the most extreme circumstances, we should be ready to litigate. A test case – unresolved at the time of writing – is the lawsuit brought in Germany by the Syrian refugee Anas Modamani against Facebook. In 2015, Modamani took a selfie with the German Chancellor Angela Merkel when he was living in a Berlin shelter, and posted it on his Facebook page. Since the terrorist attacks in Brussels in March 2016 and on the Christmas market in Berlin, the image (which Modamani has taken down) has been used repeatedly on social media and fake news sites, falsely accusing him of terrorist acts and affiliations. He hopes his lawsuit will compel Facebook to remove all posts that libel him in this way, and to compensate him accordingly each time the social network fails in this task.

The essence of the case is the gap between law and what Facebook describes as 'community standards', and who is accountable for breaches of the former. The social media giant claims that defamatory allegations are the legal responsibility of those who post them. At the hearing in Würzburg, Judge Volkmar Seipel conceded that the law had not kept pace with technological change – an important cue to legislators around the world who will have to confront this and similar problems with increasing frequency.[3] Such cases have more than intrinsic legal significance: they act as a cultural warning signal, urging action upon those in a position to address the broader questions that are raised by specific grievances.

TECHNOLOGY, HEAL THYSELF

In his letter to mark the twenty-eighth birthday of the World Wide Web, Sir Tim Berners-Lee was categorical about the duty of the tech giants to shoulder this responsibility:

> Today, most people find news and information on the web through just a handful of social media sites and search engines. These sites make more money when we click on the links they show us. And, they choose what to show us based on algorithms which learn from our personal data that they are constantly harvesting. The net result is that these sites show us content they think we'll click on – meaning that misinformation, or 'fake news', which is surprising, shocking, or designed to appeal to our biases can spread like wildfire … those with bad intentions can game the system to spread misinformation for financial or political gain.[4]

Though he firmly – and rightly – opposed 'the creation of any central bodies to decide what is "true" or not', Sir Tim urged 'gatekeepers such as Google and

Facebook' to acknowledge their responsibility as the world's most powerful distributors of information.

Perhaps to pre-empt a wave of national and supranational regulation, the mightiest tech companies and media sites have now undertaken a series of investigations to see what can be done to address the pathologies of Post-Truth. The BBC, for instance, has established a team to identify and debunk fake news in all its forms. 'The BBC can't edit the internet, but we won't stand aside either,' said its news chief, James Harding. 'We will fact-check the most popular outliers on Facebook, Instagram and other social media. We are working with Facebook, in particular, to see how we can be most effective. Where we see deliberately misleading stories masquerading as news, we'll publish a "Reality Check" that says so.'[5]

As a public service broadcaster, funded primarily by a licence fee and still trusted around the world, the BBC is in a unique position to offer a powerful (and viral) fact-checking service. It promises more 'slow news' (in-depth analysis and explanation) to balance the mayfly perspectives of the so-called 'Twitter cycle' – though, in the new media environment, its twenty-four-hour news channels will remain under immense pressure to be first, as well as right.

For the tech giants, whose revenues depend upon clicks, advertising and (in some cases) online purchases, the question of editing content was initially marginal.

Now, however, Google has established a 'Digital News Initiative', funding Full Fact to the tune of $50,000 to work on an automated fact-checking system. In January 2017, meanwhile, Facebook announced its own 'Journalism Project' that sought to 'establish stronger ties … [with] the news industry'.

Its explicit objective was to 'equip people with the knowledge they need to be informed readers in the digital age'. The social network company has also strengthened its collaboration with the First Draft Partner Network, a group of publishers and platforms collaborating to find ways of verifying content from social media. In December 2016, Facebook announced a new system that would enable a fake news story to be flagged up, triggering a verification and labelling process that would warn users to treat it with caution.

To this end, the network is already working with five independent fact-checkers: ABC News, AP, Factcheck.org, PolitiFact and Snopes.[6] Mark Zuckerberg, the founder of Facebook, has spoken of 'technical systems to detect what people will flag as false before they do it themselves' – though it is not clear how close that ambition is to being realised. In March 2017, the corporation launched a pilot scheme that alerted users attempting to share 'disputed content' and directed those seeking further information to the code of principles adopted by the International Fact-Checking Network.

Meanwhile, the parent company of Snapchat, the popular video and picture messaging app, also unveiled new guidelines to address the problem, declaring that all content in its 'Discover' channels had to be 'fact-checked and accurate', that links could not be 'deceptive, misleading or fraudulent', and that publishers could not 'impersonate or claim to be another person or entity, create a false presence for an organization, or otherwise use the content in a manner that does or is intended to mislead, confuse or deceive others'.[7]

Not to be outdone, Apple's CEO, Tim Cook, said in early 2017 that fake news was 'killing people's minds' and that tech giants, including his own, needed to work with governments to thwart its spread. 'It has to be ingrained in the schools, it has to be ingrained in the public,' Cook told the *Daily Telegraph*. 'There has to be a massive campaign. We have to think through every demographic. We need the modern version of a public-service announcement campaign. It can be done quickly if there is a will.'

As Cook conceded, however, there was a direct tension between this objective and the prevalence of clickbait. 'We are going through this period of time right here where unfortunately some of the people that are winning are the people that spend their time trying to get the most clicks, not tell the most truth.' It is also true that these undertakings by tech giants will only have teeth if public pressure is maintained: much of what is presented as corporate social responsibility is no more than spray-on virtue, Potemkin piety.[8]

At the heart of the rhetoric and showy project launches is the conviction that the Internet will heal itself – that the very algorithms currently driving traffic to fake news sites can be modified to produce the opposite effect and prevent their spread. As Charles Leadbeater, author of *We-Think*, observed in the first flush of Web 2.0, sites such as Wikipedia and open-source software schemes flourish when they attract a group of key contributors 'to ensure quality and limit vandalism', something like 'a tightly networked craft aristocracy'. Creative communities, he said, 'are not egalitarian'.[9]

In the nine years since Leadbeater's comments, however, the web has grown exponentially, as has its role as a first-stop source of information.[10] Accordingly, it has exercised a gravitational pull upon those who would control the way we think and behave. In a much discussed *Observer* article published in February 2017, the journalist Carole Cadwalladr traced the role of Robert Mercer, a billionaire computer scientist and hedge-funder, in transforming the media and information landscape. A close ally of Steve Bannon, Trump's chief strategist, Mercer is connected to Cambridge Analytica, a US data analytics company, that claims to have psychological profiles on 220 million American voters and allegedly assisted Leave.EU during the Brexit referendum campaign.

The basis of such profiles is the data freely available on social media, particularly Facebook. Tracking information on each page or feed, analytic algorithms can construct uncannily accurate psychometric portraits of individuals, their tastes, affinities and presumptions. The manipulation of propaganda can therefore be tailored not only to demographic groups but also to *individual voters*: the cumulative ambition is to shift popular mood without recourse to the clunkier tools of old-fashioned propaganda. Why bother with the ancient techniques of spin when you have roving programmes that can drop keywords and bespoke opinion into social media feeds?

Yet again, the objective is to trigger emotions, not to win an evidence-based debate. To use a word beloved by Bannon, the modern political warrior seeks to 'weaponise' fake news so that it becomes, as Cadwalladr puts it, 'a suicide bomb at the heart of our information system. Strapped to the live body of us – the mainstream media.' Propaganda methods piloted in Russia have migrated to the West and are being unleashed upon populations almost universally unaware that their social media pages are being mined for data by a new information-industrial complex.[11]

Against such plutocratic, political and algorithmic firepower, the battle to defend the truth is all the more daunting. To start with the basics: fact-checking an unimaginably huge virtual space is a task that is ultimately too great for humans, however well intentioned and industrious. Accordingly, it must eventually be mechanised. The most rudimentary step would be to grade media sources according to their established credibility, automating the function of a consumer watchdog. The worst sites would be black-listed and flagged up as such on a user's browser.

Other prospective methods are more sophisticated. Research has shown that accurate information tends to be retweeted by users who tweet often and have many followers. Algorithms can scour posts for obviously sceptical comments – a preponderance of which suggests rumour or outright falsehood. At a deeper level, the connections between those who tweet the same story can be scrutinised to see if it is spreading legitimately or with the intervention of non-human 'bots' (software that infiltrates the web to seize information, corner markets and simulate other forms of human action).[12]

Such initiatives are the digital equivalent of the old structures of authority in human interaction: they detect legitimacy in the credentials, affiliations and language of the source. But such algorithms would not pass the Turing Test – the protocols devised by the great code-breaker Alan Turing to distinguish between human intelligence and machines. Though it is easy to envisage coding that would filter out, or flag up, the most flagrantly fake news, or draw upon a huge data-base of verified knowledge against which to check posted information, a system that could detect all or most falsehoods in real time would need fully developed Artificial Intelligence – including a sensitivity to linguistic nuance, insinuation, emotional content and apparent intent. Ask a professional poker player how he spots a 'tell': the answer will be long and complicated, rooted in the deepest subtlety of human behaviour. Or recall the classic speech delivered by Christopher Walken as the mob consigliere Vincenzo Coccotti in Tony Scott's movie *True Romance* (1993):

> You know, Sicilians are great liars. The best in the world. I'm Sicilian. My father was the world heavyweight champion of Sicilian liars. From growing up with him, I learned the pantomime. There are seventeen different things a guy can do when he lies to give himself away. A guy's got seventeen pantomimes. A woman's got twenty, a guy's got seventeen. But if you know them like you know your own face, they beat lie detectors all to hell. Now, what we got here is a little game of show and tell. You don't want to show me nothing. But you're telling me everything.

Can we imagine an algorithm that could spot Coccotti's 'pantomimes'? An app that could detect a 'Sicilian liar'?

A machine that can smell the smoke from pants on fire does not exist – yet. The well-documented weaknesses of the polygraph method illustrate the inherent problems facing mechanised lie detectors.[13] That said, the pace at which AI is evolving suggests that these problems may be overcome sooner than we would suppose.

FACTS ARE NOT ENOUGH

In the meantime, *Homo sapiens* must do combat with Post-Truth. In his book on the perils of statistics, the psychologist Daniel Levitin insists that the due diligence required of today's citizens is part of 'an implicit bargain we've all made'. The trivial tasks of research and information retrieval that used to consume days can now be accomplished in seconds on a smartphone or a tablet.

'We've saved incalculable numbers of hours of trips to libraries and far-flung archives, of hunting through thick books for the one passage that will answer our question,' writes Levitin. 'The implicit bargain that we all need to make explicit is that we will use just *some* of that time we saved in information acquisition to perform proper information verification.'

He commends as a tool kit the methods devised by Thomas Bayes (1701–61), the English statistician and philosopher, whereby the probability of a proposition's truth is determined by the incremental accumulation of evidence.[14] The more a doctor learns of our symptoms, the more accurately he can diagnose our condition. The more verifiable evidence we have of President Trump's connections in Russia, the more we can say with confidence about the probity of his relationship with its government. We need to recover the patience to apply this technique.

This is a fair demand to make. But to stand a chance of success, such strategies must be advanced in the world as it is, rather than the world as it once was. In particular, as the 'backfire effect' illustrates, it is a mistake to imagine that Post-Truth will crumble under the weight of freshly verified information repeated relentlessly and ubiquitously.

Indeed, it is a common error to confuse data with truth: the former informs the latter, but they are not the same thing. In the Brexit referendum, the Remain camp's greatest mistake was to assume that torrents of statistics would win the day. In the Vietnam War, what Viktor Mayer-Schönberger and Kenneth Cukier call the 'dictatorship of data' had a disastrous impact upon US strategy. Robert McNamara, Secretary of Defense under Presidents Kennedy and Johnson, displayed an almost religious faith in the power of statistics to guide public policy. As a consequence, the daily 'body count' – the number of enemy dead – became the crucial 'data point'.

Privately, and later publicly, the generals believed this statistic to be a useless measure of success in such a complex military and political context. Its centrality to the debate also invited fabrication: officers in the field were alleged to have inflated the figures as a matter of course. The truth of battle could not be captured in a spreadsheet or a set of graphs – any more than the case for Britain's continued membership of the EU could be reduced to a series of statistics.[15]

In the right circumstances, a lie may be defeated by the skilful deployment of facts. But Post-Truth is, first and foremost, an emotional phenomenon. It concerns our attitude to truth, rather than truth itself.

From this, it should be clear that the counter-attack has to be emotionally intelligent as well as rigorously rational. In their account of science denial, Sara and Jack Gorman insist that academics and researchers must raise their game accordingly in the public sphere. Just as the opponents of vaccination have deployed the techniques of celebrity, so 'scientifically credible charismatic leaders' are needed to counter their claims.[16] At a time when Professor Brian Cox can sell out stadiums, the British astronaut Tim Peake is mobbed by fans and Professor Stephen Hawking is a cultural icon, this is not an unreasonable expectation. As the Gormans put it:

We propose that scientists not only become fluent in the kind of information we confront on the Internet but also that they join the conversation in a much more active way. We think that scientific and medical societies in particular have much to gain from formalizing a broad, far-reaching online and social media strategy. Yes, all scientific and medical societies these days have websites and send out e-newsletters and digitize their journals. But how many of them have a truly active Twitter or Facebook account providing up-to-the-minute coverage for the general public about important scientific and medical issues?

Rapid rebuttal is only the start, though. As they acknowledge:

Discussion should center on not only how to make the material accessible but also how to present it in a manner that will discourage irrational response … Instead of just telling people the percent risk, scientists need to understand what these percentages actually mean to people and, most important, frame them in a way that they will be most convincing and acceptable to the nonscientists. A small amount of training in cognitive psychology and behavioral economics should make scientists more aware of the biases and heuristics people use to interpret scientific information and teach them how to communicate around these psychological processes …

In a Post-Truth world, in other words, it is not enough to make an intellectual case. In many (perhaps most) contexts, facts need to be communicated in a way that recognises emotional as well as rational imperatives. For doctors talking to patients, for instance, one such model is 'Motivation Interviewing', a clinical method developed in addiction treatment that goes beyond the simple transference of information to explore the subject's motives, anxieties and ambivalence to encourage behavioural change. At a time when most British family doctors spend an average of seven to eight minutes per patient, this is an ambitious proposal.[17] But something like it will be necessary to deal definitively with the propaganda onslaughts of – for instance – the anti-vaccine lobby.

It is important, too, to understand the multiplicity of methods available to those propagating lies. In China, state-sponsored commenters – millions of them – fabricate about 448 million social media posts a year. But, as one study has shown,

> the Chinese regime's strategy is to avoid arguing with skeptics of the party and the government, and to not even discuss controversial issues. We infer that the goal of this massive secretive operation is instead to regularly distract the public and change the subject, as most of these posts involve cheerleading for China, the revolutionary history of the Communist Party or other symbols of the regime.[18]

If distraction can be the enemy of truth, it follows that its protectors must engage in the battle for attention. It is not enough to issue a press release, appear on a news channel or tweet a correction. The *means* of correction have to match the prevailing culture. A viral podcast, a demonstration or an online petition may do more to banish a falsehood than a straightforward assertion of fact. This is a slippery slope, of course: an endless battle of distraction and counter-distraction would do nothing for democratic discourse. Veracity must never be compromised by theatricality. But it is naive to think that the battle against Post-Truth will be won with sole recourse to the routine techniques of verification.

TRUMP THE NARRATIVE

Progress is sequential: which is to say, those who hope for change, or to combat a pernicious social trend, must adapt with steely discipline to the circumstances in which they find themselves. This is less obvious than it seems. There is a powerful instinct simply to reinstate that which is lost or jeopardised, to reassert the status quo ante. But, as I said at the beginning of this chapter, those who wish to defend Enlightenment values in this transformed context – hectic mobility, technological revolution, emotional ferment – must operate within its parameters. All else is delusion.

In his book *The Myth Gap*, Alex Evans argues that 'we need new myths that speak about who we are and the world we inhabit'.[19] It has, of course, become commonplace to use the word 'myth' as a synonym for 'familiar falsehood'. But this is not what Evans is championing. Addressing the specific case of climate change science, he argues that technocratic language, statistics, acronyms and opaque strategy documents can do as much to deter public recognition of reality as to advance it. For those seeking to animate support, 'a really resonant story is the spark that lights the movement's flame'.[20] In other words: the battle between feeling and rationality is, to some extent, a false dichotomy. More than ever, truth requires an emotional delivery system that speaks to experience, memory and hope.

Indeed, the very idea that truth needs to be defended has a mythic dimension. From the theft of fire by Prometheus, via Odin's sacrifice of his eye in return for wisdom, to the much more recent genre of the detective novel, the determined quest for knowledge – often at a price – has been one of the great archetypes of the human story. It is not absurd to imagine a modern, mythic appeal to mankind's collective yearning for certitude and honesty – not in the crass, conspiratorial language of the so-called 'Truthers', but in an open, collaborative rebellion against the cognitive sickness of our times.

The very word 'narrative' has been contaminated by overuse in the political world as a faddish alternative to 'strategy' or 'plan'. But this should not deter us from exploring its core meaning and its central relevance to the Post-Truth era. Narrative – defined as a spoken or written account of connected elements – is essential to the fightback called for in this book.

Today's truth-teller must speak to head and heart alike. By this, I do not mean that press reports should be written in the idiom of fiction, or that financial analysts must now speak in iambic pentameters. This is not a call for emotional slush, touchy-feely outpourings or New Age news. Truth must always have a serrated edge.

My point – manifest, I hope, throughout these pages – is that veracity will be drowned out unless it is resonant. To take a current example: listing the lies that Trump tells is hugely important, but it isn't enough. His success has been built upon a story as powerful as it is simple: that he can 'Make America Great Again'. He has appealed not to verifiable data, but to grievances and fears – what business gurus call 'inadequacy marketing'.[21]

To defend the truth against the President and those who will follow his lead, powerful counter-narratives are required; stories that, in the words of the branding entrepreneur Jonah Sachs, call 'their listeners to growth and maturity' rather than irrationality and huddled fear of conspiracy.[22] This approach – so-called 'empowerment marketing' – trades Freud's emphasis upon pathology and neurosis for the psychological theories of Abraham Maslow (1908–70), a former president of the American Psychological Association and co-founder of the *Journal of Humanistic Psychology*.

Maslow is best known for his 'hierarchy of needs', a pyramidal structure that identified human requirements beyond basic survival and a sense of deficiency. Human beings, he contended, yearn for more than a bearable existence. They mature, with differing degrees of success, towards the satisfaction of deeper needs: wholeness, perfection, justice, richness, simplicity, beauty, truth, uniqueness and playfulness.

The relevance of this analysis is its courageous but necessary insistence upon treating those with whom we interact – voters, readers, viewers, social media users – as adults. It appeals not only to self-interest and convenience, but also to human agency and maturity. It is a much harder path than the populist promise of instant success, imagined enemies crushed and inconvenient truths ignored – but all the better for that.

Here are three examples of what such counter-narratives might look like. First, there is the speech delivered by Harvey Milk – one of the first openly gay elected officials in the US – in San Diego on 10 March 1978:

> The only thing they have to look forward to is hope. And you have to give them hope. Hope for a better world, hope for a better tomorrow, hope for a better place to come to if the pressures at home are too great. Hope that all will be all right. Without hope, not only gays, but the blacks, the seniors, the handicapped, the us'es, the us'es will give up. And if you help elect to the central

committee and more offices, more gay people, that
gives a green light to all who feel disenfranchised, a
green light to move forward. It means hope to a nation
that has given up, because if a gay person makes it, the
doors are open to everyone.[23]

The deftness of Milk's rhetoric was rooted in a slightly
clunky word: the 'us'es'. What he meant to express was
that a modern pluralist society was composed of multiple communities that could co-exist, driven by the
hope of a better life in negotiated harmony – or not.
His narrative was driven not by a sense of entitlement
but by a rejection of despair and a call to action.

Second: in his great essay 'The Power of the Powerless'
(1978), Václav Havel, later to become the President of
the Czech Republic, encapsulated a message of resilience
in a single metaphor. 'There are times,' he said, 'when
we must sink to the bottom of our misery to understand truth just as we must descend to the bottom of a
well to see the stars in broad daylight.'[24] In a separate
context, he beautifully mythologised man's capacity to
combat falsehood: 'The deeper the experience of an
absence of meaning – in other words of absurdity – the
more energetically meaning is sought.'[25]

Third, and most recently, Danny Boyle's opening
ceremony at the London 2012 Olympics gave narrative force to the social complexities of Britishness, the
nation's eccentric brew of tradition and modernity, core

values and historical diversity. The extravaganza celebrated the NHS, 1942 Beveridge Report on welfare and immigration, but also saluted the ancestral achievements of the Armed Forces, cherished hymns and the Union of England, Scotland, Wales and Northern Ireland. The governing theme of the show was the indomitable spirit of invention and innovation: the notion of Britain as revolutionary country, whose revolution was not political but scientific, intellectual and creative.[26]

A year before the ceremony, riots had erupted in the cities of England. Four years after this celebration of confident pluralism, Britain voted, as if contrarily, for Brexit. What Boyle achieved was scarcely the last word on what his country stood, and stands, for. But – like the rhetoric of Milk and Havel – it showed what can be done to assert reality in the form of stories, and with what panache.

For those who would win back the voters that were driven to support Trump or Brexit by a sense of disenfranchisement, the mission is both clear and daunting. They must find an alternative to the 'deep story' of disillusionment described in Chapter 1, acknowledging the anxieties of those who feel left behind without appeasing the bigotries fed by this disquiet.

Such a counter-narrative must be constructed with great delicacy. It needs to take account of the alienation spawned by the pace of global change, without deceiving the public that this pace is likely to slow.

Population mobility, for example, is not going to decrease significantly, in spite of populist claims to the contrary. What is required now is a discourse rooted in generous confidence, not tribal fear, one that emphasises the benefits of well-managed immigration and recognises that admission to a country entails responsibilities to integrate as well as rights to be treated unequivocally as a fully fledged citizen.

In the UK, Sir Oliver Letwin was right to observe in November 2016 that the main parties had 'made a terrible mistake' in failing to argue, with commitment and resolve, that 'properly controlled migration enriches the country in every sense'.[27]

This mistake is by no means impossible to correct. Though Angela Merkel's statesmanlike admission of Syrian refugees has proved controversial, Germany has shown greater sophistication than other European nations in its approach to immigration – emphasising not only its economic benefits but also its social value, confronting directly the notion that it is *kein Einwanderungsland* ('not a country of immigration').[28]

The defeat of the far Right candidate, Geert Wilders, in the Dutch election of March 2017 shows that the global advance of Post-Truth populism is not preordained. But those who would fight back must display humility and honesty: the humility to listen and the honesty to treat voters as mature citizens.

Inequality, housing shortages, failing schools and health crises are all causes for legitimate grievances, but they will not be addressed by closed borders, or even partial reductions in immigration. Slogans such as 'Take Back Control' and 'Make America Great Again' may have won votes, but are also insultingly hollow.

The task for those who do not share the politics of Trump or the Brexiteers is to speak with empathy and candour, to wrap facts in stories that speak to ordinary human concerns. Narrative must never violate or embellish truth; it should be its most powerful vehicle.

SO TRUE, FUNNY HOW IT SEEMS

Ridicule is another force that debunks lies, but does so with emotional impact rather than an intellectual battering ram. In her book on the David Irving trial, Deborah Lipstadt recalls the thesis of her lawyer, Anthony Julius: 'To defeat your adversary and bury him is one thing. To dress him in a jester's costume and have him perform for you is another, more crushing blow. He survives to give witness to his own powerlessness.' This, she reflects, was the importance of her battle: 'Repeatedly during the trial, David Irving was left exposed, not just as a falsifier of history, but as an irrational and foolish figure.' In the same way, she argues, Charlie Chaplin's *The Great Dictator* and Mel Brooks's

The Producers reduce Hitler to a figure of absurdity – belittling him, as well as branding him evil.[29]

As noted in the previous chapter, the best satirists can – and do – act as picadors in the fight against Post-Truth. When Congressman Bill Posey of Florida introduced a bill into the House of Representatives in 2009 requiring presidential candidates to produce their birth certificates – an attempt to enshrine the 'Birther' controversy in US legislation – Comedy Central's Stephen Colbert challenged him to produce DNA evidence to 'quell the persistent rumors' that 'Florida congressmen are part alligator. I have had enough with the reckless whispering!'[30] Posey was mortified: 'I expected there would be some civil debate about it, but it wasn't civil. Just a bunch of name-calling and personal denigration. … There is no reason to say that I'm the illegitimate grandson of an alligator.' Maybe not – but the experience compelled him to declare that he had 'no reason to question' Obama's birthplace.[31] Posey's bill – H.R. 1503 – died when Congress adjourned in 2010.

In fact, Colbert had already bestowed upon what would later become known as Post-Truth his own name: 'truthiness'. As he explained in a 2006 interview:

Truthiness is tearing apart our country, and I don't mean the argument over who came up with the word. I don't know whether it's a new thing, but it's certainly a current thing, in that it doesn't seem to matter what facts are. It used to be, everyone was entitled to their own opinion, but not their own facts. But that's not the case anymore. Facts matter not at all. Perception is everything. It's certainty. People love the president [George W. Bush] because he's certain of his choices as a leader, even if the facts that back him up don't seem to exist. It's the fact that he's certain that is very appealing to a certain section of the country. I really feel a dichotomy in the American populace. What is important? What you want to be true, or what *is* true?[32]

As argued earlier, President Trump has answered Colbert's rhetorical question by replacing the standards of public life with the criteria of success in show business. But this, of course, makes him all the more sensitive to the barbs of satirists whom he regards – subconsciously or otherwise – as fellow entertainers. His fixation with *Saturday Night Live* (and Alec Baldwin's impression of him) has been especially revealing.

On 4 December 2016, in the midst of his faltering transition, the President-elect tweeted: 'Just tried watching *Saturday Night Live* – unwatchable! Totally biased, not funny and the Baldwin impersonation just can't get any worse. Sad.' Only five days before his inauguration, he had time to renew the attack: '.@NBCNews is bad but *Saturday Night Live* is the worst of NBC. Not funny, cast is terrible, always a complete hit job. Really bad television!' To an extent, Trump is right to be bothered: the forces that created him could yet destroy him. A politician so dependent upon emotional resonance cannot afford to become a figure of general ridicule. Clearly, the satirists are doing their job. What about the rest of us?

THE TRUTH – IF WE CAN KEEP IT

In *Apocalypse Now*, Marlon Brando as Colonel Kurtz asks Martin Sheen's Willard to tell his son all he has seen at his Cambodian compound: 'Everything I did, everything you saw, because there's nothing that I detest more than the stench of lies. And if you understand me, Willard, you will do this for me.'

As dubious a role model as Kurtz surely is, he reminds us that lies contaminate all they touch – including, in his case, basic sanity. The greatest peril of the Post-Truth era is that our sense of smell has failed us. We have become indifferent or inured to 'the stench of lies', resigned to the malodorous atmosphere of competing truth claims. To put it another way: the flames of democratic collapse are not yet consuming our society. But our collective smoke alarm is faulty.

Conceivably, it may be reactivated by the experiences that lie ahead. As we have seen, Umberto Eco argued that realism would always reassert itself when we encountered 'lines of resistance'. We cannot walk through walls, survive underwater without oxygen, or drive through a dead-end. Politics and culture have their equivalents. The votes for Brexit and for Trump were fed by reactionary sentiment but also – definitively – by an insistence upon *change*.

Whatever else happens in this particular presidency and this particular rearrangement of Britain's relationship with the rest of Europe, the expectations raised on both sides of the Atlantic cannot possibly be satisfied. When the promise of transformation fails and the public encounters its own 'lines of resistance' – a moment of maximum social danger – it will be a civic duty of great urgency to assert the value of truth in political debate.

What cannot be assumed is that this will happen of its own accord, as an organic response to disenchantment. If anything, political disappointment is the handmaiden of Post-Truth, a solvent of trust and a cue to further tribal huddling. The task cannot wait. It is much too pressing to be postponed *sine die*. If the truth is to reclaim its position of priority in our culture, we must put it there.

At the heart of this challenge is the notion of citizenship. In two specific respects, the twentieth century eroded that ancient concept of conjoined rights and responsibilities. In spite of persistent revisionist claims to the contrary, the dramatic expansion of the state after the Second World War was necessary as a civilising force to enable the spread of education, healthcare and welfare provision. If anything, twenty-first-century conservatives are rediscovering the merits of government – at least in principle – after decades of promises to 'roll back its frontiers'.[33] But there is no denying the flipside of the state's growth in the past seventy years – which is the partial infantilisation of the public it serves. As much as the modern electorate despises politicians, it still turns to them reflexively for solutions to everything. Our instinctive response to a problem is to say: 'they should do something about that'. But who are 'they'? 'They' used to be 'us'.

This delegation of civic responsibility to the very political class we claim to deplore has been compounded by a quite distinct trend, most associated with, though not confined to, governments of the centre-Right. The reframing of public services as retail products, and of patients, parents and passengers as customers has not only blurred the boundary between the state and the private sector. It has also made citizenship increasingly indistinguishable from consumerism. What are euphemistically called 'flexible labour practices', zero-hour contracts and the rise of the gig economy, have tended to strip work of its centrality to human experience. The conventions of the lifetime career are long gone. Automation and outsourcing now threaten the very future of work – or so it seems.

What remains is *consumption*: no bad thing in itself, until it starts to define us. When the things you can buy online matter more to you than the things you can do in your neighbourhood; when you communicate with the social media 'friends' you never meet more than you see your real friends; when your notion of the 'public space' is confined to the screen in your hand: all this removes the sinew from citizenship. It encourages the passivity that is so important to Post-Truth.

Statesmanship can make and has made a difference. Franklin Roosevelt's fireside chats were an appeal to civic spirit, rooted in an insistence upon the sovereignty of truth. As he put it on 27 May 1941: 'The pressing problems that confront us are military and naval problems. We cannot afford to approach them from the point of view of wishful thinkers or sentimentalists. What we face is cold, hard fact.'[34]

Sound public policy can play a part in the resistance to Post-Truth. It is encouraging, for instance, that the Culture, Media and Sport Select Committee of the House of Commons, under the chairmanship of Damian Collins MP, has been swift to launch an inquiry into fake news and its 'threat to democracy'.[35]

The 'Nudge' school of behavioural economics has also shown that government can steer citizens away from misinformation towards fact-based decisions – about health, personal finance, the environment and nutrition – through encouragement rather than the blunt instrument of legislation and regulation.[36] It has been argued, more provocatively, that there are cases when government has a duty to ignore the objections of the misinformed minority – a duty often cited in the case of compulsory fluoridation and to take action 'mandating protection from the dangers of misinformed activity'.[37] But even the most ardent champions of Jeffersonian democracy concede that there is no glibly paternalistic answer to Post-Truth.[38]

Indeed, how could there be? Leadership may be a necessary condition of change. But – especially in an age of distrust – it is no longer sufficient (if it ever was, at least in democratic societies). As Martin Luther King wrote in his 'Letter from Birmingham Jail' (1963), indifference is the greatest challenge to those who speak the truth:

> The Negro's great stumbling block in his stride toward freedom is not the White Citizen's Councilor or the Ku Klux Klanner, but the white moderate, who is more devoted to 'order' than to justice; who prefers a negative peace which is the absence of tension to a positive peace which is the presence of justice; who constantly says, 'I agree with you in the goal you seek, but I cannot agree with your methods of direct action.' … Shallow understanding from people of good will is more frustrating than absolute misunderstanding from people of ill will. Lukewarm acceptance is much more bewildering than outright rejection.[39]

In a few majestic sentences, King captured the principal psychological barrier that confronts any agent of change. The story of mankind is the story of the battle between indifference and commitment, *within* people as well as between them. For many, conformity is the default position. The parapet is there for a reason: so you don't stick your head above it. Inertia is the safe option – until it isn't. Which is to say that we often regret our earlier passivity only when it is too late.

Of this much we can be sure. The renewal of citizenship will not be imposed from above. If people want an end to the Post-Truth era, they must will it themselves. If, having encountered its disagreeable consequences (Eco's 'lines of resistance'), they want a change, they must demand it. The phrase 'people power' has been debased by overuse, but it is not without meaning. In John le Carré's novel *The Secret Pilgrim*, the veteran spymaster George Smiley spells out the facts of the matter to a youthful audience:

> It was *man* who ended the Cold War in case you didn't notice. It wasn't weaponry, or technology, or armies or campaigns. It was just *man*. Not even Western man either, as it happened, but our sworn enemy in the East, who went into the streets, faced the bullets and the batons and said: we've had enough … And the ideologies trailed after these

impossible events like condemned prisoners, as
ideologies do when they've had their day.[40]

There is no romance in this. The revolution of 1989
was the end of a seventy-two-year nightmare, a long haul
of cataclysmic suffering, oppression and vanquished
resistance. Apartheid exacted an astonishing cost before
its fall. And not all popular movements end well, or
coherently: one has only to think of the Prague Spring
of 1968 or its Arab counterpart in 2011.

But Smiley's point stands. The only reliable engines of
change are citizens themselves. The US Republican Party
would not have been transformed as it has been without the organisational power of the Tea Party. The UK
Labour Party would not have shifted as it has to the Left
without the grass-roots energy of the group Momentum. The respective impact of the Occupy movement
and Jubilee Debt Campaign is also instructive.

Whatever you think of these specific movements,
concentrate upon the form, rather than the content.
It is not hard to imagine a similar, loose-knit alliance
arising in response to Post-Truth and to the damage it
is already doing to our civic fabric: #TellUsTheTruth.
The clarion-call 'don't mourn – organise!' is usually
associated with the Left. But its application need not be
confined to any particular ideology.

At the very least, we must affirm the truth in a
commanding fashion, instead of merely repeating

the lie by denying it. Rationality should be matched by imagination and innovation. If Post-Truth is to be defied and defeated, the endeavour must be collective, sustained and stubborn. There will be setbacks, twists and turns, and moments of exasperation. But if the truth still matters to us as a civilisation this is not a task we can shirk.

As stated in the Preface, it is an error to assume that apathy is inevitable. The greatest orators have always grasped that people respect those who have the honesty to admit the difficulty of an undertaking and to promise 'blood, toil, tears and sweat'. What makes the Gettysburg Address so extraordinary – apart from its brevity – is Lincoln's seamless rhetorical glide from humility before the fallen to a formidable national challenge: 'the great task remaining before us that, from these honoured dead we take increased devotion to that cause for which they here, gave the last full measure of devotion that we here highly resolve these dead shall not have died in vain; that the nation, shall have a new birth of freedom, and that government of the people, by the people, for the people, shall not perish from the earth.'

Consider, similarly, Churchill's genius – long before he became a war leader – for exhortation to action, founded upon a recognition that action is rarely easy. In *My Early Life* (1930), he had this to say to the young:

You have not an hour to lose. You must take your places
in life's fighting line ... Don't be content with things as
they are. 'The earth is yours and the fullness thereof'.
Enter upon your inheritance, accept your responsibilities
... You will make all kind of mistakes; but as long as you
are generous and true, and also fierce, you cannot hurt
the world or even seriously distress her.[41]

Generous, true and fierce: a model worth aspiring to.
Once again, Martin Luther King provides a relevant
text, on this occasion, in the 1965 Sermon at Temple
Israel of Hollywood. In this instance, like Churchill, he
simultaneously identifies adversity and the moral case
for confronting it:

the arc of the moral universe is long but it bends toward
justice. We shall overcome because Carlyle is right: 'No
lie can live forever.' We shall overcome because William
Cullen Bryant is right: 'Truth crushed to earth will rise
again.' We shall overcome because James Russell
Lowell is right: 'Truth forever on the scaffold, wrong
forever on the throne. Yet, that scaffold sways the future
and behind the dim unknown standeth God within the
shadow, keeping watch above his own.'[42]

Try to imagine a contemporary politician defending
the truth in such language or with such passion; or a
US President declaring: 'Ask not what your country

can do for you – ask what you can do for your country.'[43] In the long decay of public discourse that has finally brought us to the Post-Truth era, the political class and the electorate have conspired in the cheapening and enfeebling of what they say to one another. Unattainable promises are matched by unreasonable expectations; unachieved objectives are part-concealed by euphemism and evasion; the gap between rhetoric and reality breeds disenchantment and distrust. And then the cycle begins again. Who dares be honest? And who dares pay heed to honesty?

This is not an appeal to sentimentality, but precisely the opposite. It is a call to arms, a reminder that truth is discovered not distributed, that it is an ideal to be pursued not an entitlement to be lazily expected. Our demands as citizens to be told the truth must be tempered by reason but not tamed by complacency. Our insistence must be relentless.

In his clarifying remarks on the meaning of *Nineteen Eighty-Four* – a statement made not long before his death, that amounted to a valedictory message – Orwell issued a categorical warning: 'The moral to be drawn from this dangerous nightmare situation is a simple one: Don't let it happen. It depends on you.'

There was no idealism in these last words, only the hard-won realism of a writer who had dedicated his life to truth and understood that, in the end, it is only the vigilant citizen that stands watch over a free society and its fundamental values. In this struggle, there is no cavalry worth waiting for. And this, at least, has always been so. After the Constitutional Convention of 1787 in Philadelphia had ended, Benjamin Franklin was approached by a woman who asked what kind of government had been decided upon. Franklin replied: 'A republic, madam – if you can keep it.'[44]

What he meant was that a system free of the distorting forces that lead inexorably to tyranny of one kind or another is only as strong as those who protect it. Today, those forces are more complex, various and insidious than even the inventor and scientist Franklin could have imagined. But his pithy challenge remains the right one, speaking across the centuries from the age of the Founding Fathers to the precarious, cacophonous terrain of our times. It is a challenge worth meeting. Courage, persistence and collaborative spirit will be rewarded: the truth will out.

ACKNOWLEDGEMENTS

It is the literal truth that this book would not have been written – not by me, anyway – without the life-saving surgery of Adrian Steger and his team at University Hospital Lewisham. I thank them from the bottom of my heart.

My second debt is to Andrew Goodfellow, an editor of magnificence who believes in ideas, intellectual exchange and their relationship to everyday life. It was my great good fortune to work with him, and with his colleagues at Ebury: Sarah Bennie, Clarissa Pabi, Laura Horsley, Michelle Warner, Richard Collins and Ruth Killick. David Eldridge at Two Associates did a terrific job on the cover.

My agent nonpareil, Caroline Michel, is an inspiration as well as a true friend and mentor. I thank her and her colleagues at Peters Fraser and Dunlop, Kate Evans and Tessa David.

Many friends acted as cheerleaders, morale-boosters and guides: Sarah and Johnnie Standing, Dylan Jones, Sir Evelyn de Rothschild, D-J Collins, John Cleese,

Julia Hobsbawm, Tessa Jowell (who was kind enough to show me the invaluable lecture notes on Post-Truth she had used while teaching at Harvard), Sarah Sands, John Patten, Jane Miles, Matthew Norman, Andy Coulson, Melissa Kite, Martin Ivens and Anne McElvoy, Sir Craig Oliver, Rafael Behr and Simon Mason.

As always, my greatest debt is to my family: my brothers, Pad and Mick, have given me unstinting support. It is amazing to me that my sons, Zac and Teddy, are now teenagers (and taller than me): they are, and will always be, the heart of my life.

After nearly half a century, my dad is still an endlessly generous source of wisdom, patience, humour and love – and a hero to me. I cannot thank him enough.

This book is dedicated to my beloved mum, who was as committed to truth as anyone I have ever known. I miss her and think of her every day.

NOTES

PREFACE

1 An objective achieved: see http://www.standard.co.uk/comment/
comment/matthew-dancona-donald-trump-s-victory-will-be-as-
great-a-test-for-theresa-may-as-brexit-a3391521.html

2 Sonia Orwell and Ian Angus (eds), *The Collected Essays of
George Orwell*, Vol. II: *My Country Right or Left 1940–43*
(1980 paperback edition), pp. 295–6.

1. 'WHO CARES?'

1 At the time of writing http://www.politifact.com/personalities/
donald-trump/

2 http://www.bbc.co.uk/news/uk-37995600

3 https://www.thenation.com/article/post-truth-and-its-
consequences-what-a-25-year-old-essay-tells-us-about-the-
current-moment/

4 http://grist.org/article/2010-03-30-post-truth-politics/

5 https://www.washingtonpost.com/politics/2016/live-updates/
general-election/real-time-fact-checking-and-analysis-of-the-
first-presidential-debate/fact-check-has-trump-declared-
bankruptcy-four-or-six-times/?utm_term=.7896ea11aa1b

6 http://www.ngca.co.uk/docs/Barthes_WorldOfWrestling.pdf

7   http://uk.businessinsider.com/sean-spicer-berates-media-over-inauguration-crowd-size-coverage-2017-1?r=US&IR=T

8   http://www.independent.co.uk/news/world/americas/kellyanne-conway-sean-spicer-alternative-facts-lies-press-briefing-donald-trump-administration-a7540441.html

9   For Trump's relationship with Cohn, see Michael Kranish and Marc Fisher, *Trump Revealed: An American Journey of Ambition, Ego, Money and Power* (2016).

10 http://www.politico.com/magazine/story/2017/01/donald-trump-lies-liar-effect-brain-214658

11 On the importance of stories to contests of all kinds, see Jonah Sachs, *Winning the Story Wars: Why Those Who Tell – and Live – the Best Stories Will Rule the Future* (2012).

12 http://www.nbcnews.com/politics/donald-trump/trump-s-electoral-college-win-was-not-biggest-reagan-n722016

13 https://www.theatlantic.com/international/archive/2016/11/brexit-plus-plus-plus/507107/

14 https://www.theguardian.com/politics/2016/jun/29/leave-donor-plans-new-party-to-replace-ukip-without-farage

15 http://www.strongerin.co.uk/get_the_facts#x98pwVEjauDdjZrt.97

16 This and other quotes from Cummings: https://dominiccummings.wordpress.com/2017/01/09/on-the-referendum-21-branching-histories-of-the-2016-referendum-and-the-frogs-before-the-storm-2/

17 http://www.huffingtonpost.co.uk/entry/evan-davis-newsnight-bbc-daniel-hannan-mep-eu-referendum-brexit_uk_576e2967e4b08d2c56393241

18 http://www.huffingtonpost.co.uk/entry/daniel-hannan-mep-bbc-newsnight-evan-davis-vote-leave-immigration_uk_576e723de4b08d2c5639423a

19 https://www.theguardian.com/politics/2016/jun/16/nigel-farage-defends-ukip-breaking-point-poster-queue-of-migrants

20 http://www.telegraph.co.uk/news/2016/06/21/eu-referendum-final-opinion-poll-shows-remain-surge-as-claims-su/

21 http://blogs.lse.ac.uk/politicsandpolicy/immigration-demons-and-academic-evidence/

22 http://mediterraneanaffairs.com/april-16-referendum-turkey-europe/

23 https://fullfact.org/europe/our-eu-membership-fee-55-million/

24 http://www.independent.co.uk/news/business/news/eu-referendum-statistics-regulator-loses-patience-with-leave-campaign-over-350m-a-week-eu-cost-a7051756.html

25 http://www.independent.co.uk/news/uk/politics/brexit-350-million-a-week-extra-for-the-nhs-only-an-aspiration-says-vote-leave-campaigner-chris-a7105246.html

26 https://www.theguardian.com/politics/2016/jun/26/eu-referendum-brexit-vote-leave-iain-duncan-smith-nhs

27 http://www.newstatesman.com/politics/uk/2016/06/how-brexit-campaign-lied-us-and-got-away-it

28 http://www2.politicalbetting.com/index.php/archives/2017/01/30/polling-matters-opinium-survey-public-backs-brexit-as-the-right-decision-by-52-to-39-as-opposition-softens/

29 http://www.reuters.com/article/us-britain-eu-poll-idUSKBN15L231?il=0

30 http://www.usatoday.com/story/opinion/2017/02/17/trump-executive-orders-elite-popular-polls-muslim-ban-immigration-column/97920456/

31 Ralph Keyes, *The Post-Truth Era: Dishonesty and Deception in Contemporary Life* (2004), p. 25.

32 Ibid., p. 48.

33 http://content.time.com/time/specials/packages/article/0,28804,1859513_1859526,00.html

34 http://www.historyinink.com/0060502_Harry_S_Truman_TLS_10-5-1960.htm

35 http://www.nytimes.com/1988/10/16/books/with-the-bark-off.html?pagewanted=all

36 As quoted in John Dean, *The Rehnquist Choice: The Untold Story of the Nixon Appointment That Redefined the Supreme Court* (2001).

37 Ibid., p. 126.

38 Ibid., p. 69, my emphasis.

39 There is an extensive literature on political mendacity, including: Christopher Hitchens, *No One Left to Lie to: The Values of the Worst Family* (1999), Peter Oborne, *The Rise of Political Lying* (2005), and Robert Hutton, *Would They Lie to You? How to Spin Friends and Manipulate People* (2014).

40 https://www.ft.com/content/0f70a060-c842-11dc-94a6-0000779fd2ac

41 https://www.nytimes.com/2016/11/06/magazine/the-party-that-wants-to-make-poland-great-again.html

42 Peter Pomerantsev, *Nothing Is True and Everything Is Possible* (2016 paperback edition), pp. 271–2.

43 https://www.theguardian.com/world/commentisfree/2016/dec/19/trump-putin-same-side-new-world-order

44 http://www.independent.co.uk/news/people/donald-trump-president-michael-moore-warning-biggest-f-you-in-human-history-a7406311.html

45 See Arlie Russell Hochschild, *Strangers in Their Own Land: Anger and Mourning on the American Right* (2016), Chapter 9.

46 Two influential texts typical of this school of thought: Daniel Kahneman, *Thinking, Fast and Slow* (2011); and Richard H. Thaler and Cass R. Sunstein, *Nudge: Improving Decisions about Health, Wealth, and Happiness* (2008).

47 See Daniel Goleman, *Emotional Intelligence: Why It Can Matter More Than IQ* (1995).

48 Drew Westen, *The Political Brain* (2007); and Daniel H. Pink, *A Whole New Mind: Why Right-Brainers Will Rule the Future* (2005).

49 Keyes, op. cit., p. 115.

50 David Brooks, *Bobos in Paradise: The New Upper Class and How They Got There* (2001), p. 250.

51 Keyes, op. cit., pp. 187ff.

52 Ibid., p. 117.

2. 'YOU CAN'T HANDLE THE TRUTH!'

1 http://www.huffingtonpost.co.uk/entry/michael-gove-experts-economists-andrew-marr-obr-ifs-nigel-farage_uk_583abe45e4b0207d19184080

2 Francis Fukuyama, *Trust: The Social Virtues and the Creation of Prosperity* (1995). See also: Stephen M. R. Covey with Rebecca R. Merrill, *The Speed of Trust: The One Thing That Changes Everything* (2006); Anthony Seldon with Kunal Khatri, *Trust: How We Lost It and How to Get It Back* (2009); and Julia Hobsbawm (ed.), *Where the Truth Lies: Trust and Morality in the Business of PR, Journalism and Communications* (2010 revised second edition).

3 T. Goertzel. 'Belief in conspiracy theories', *Political Psychology*, 15 (4) (1994), pp. 731–42.

4 For a heroic defence of globalisation and much else, see Matt Ridley, *The Evolution of Everything: How Ideas Emerge* (2015).

5 https://www.ft.com/content/fa332f58-d9bf-11e6-944b-e7eb37a6aa8e

6 http://www.bbc.co.uk/news/education-38557838

7 See Ari Rabin-Havt and Media Matters, *Lies Incorporated: The World of Post-Truth Politics* (2016); Naomi Oreskes and Erik M. Conway, *Merchants of Doubt: How a Handful of*

Scientists Obscured the Truth on Issues from Tobacco Smoke to Global Warming (2010); and Michael Specter, *Denialism: How Irrational Thinking Prevents Scientific Progress, Harms the Planet and Threatens Our Lives* (2009).

8 Rabin-Havt, op. cit., pp. 5–6.

9 Ibid., pp. 43–4.

10 As editor of the *Spectator*, I was embroiled in one such controversy over climate change science. See https://www.theguardian.com/commentisfree/cif-green/2009/sep/14/climate-change-denial and http://blogs.spectator.co.uk/2009/09/an-empty-chair-for-monbiot/

11 Rabin-Havt, op cit., pp. 50–51.

12 See Rob Brotherton, *Suspicious Minds: Why We Believe Conspiracy Theories* (2016 paperback), p. 233.

13 This was certainly the conclusion I drew when I made two BBC Radio 4 documentaries in 2007 on the potential of the new technology. For a synopsis see this *Spectator* article: http://www.spectator.co.uk/2007/11/the-mighty-should-quake-before-the-wiki-man/. For a fine exploration of this potential, see Charles Leadbeater, *We-Think: The Power of Mass Creativity* (2008).

14 http://webfoundation.org/2017/03/web-turns-28-letter/

15 Bernard Williams, *Truth and Truthfulness: An Essay in Genealogy* (2004 paperback edition), p. 216.

16 See Henry Farrell, 'The consequences of the Internet for politics', *Annual Review of Political Science* (2012).

17 See Malcolm Nance, *The Plot to Hack America: How Putin's Cyberspies and WikiLeaks Tried to Steal the 2016 Election* (2016).

18 See Tim Wu, *The Attention Merchants: From the Daily Newspaper to Social Media, How our Time and Attention is Harvested and Sold* (2016).

19 Eric S. Raymond, *The Cathedral and the Bazaar: Musings on Linux and Open Source by an Accidental Revolutionary* (1999).

20 https://www.buzzfeed.com/craigsilverman/top-fake-news-of-2016?utm_term=.dvv3pRNPm4#.qvMbB39LyN

21 https://www.buzzfeed.com/craigsilverman/fake-news-survey?utm_term=.poNY8E5Vwo#.fjQKeXzQ75

22 https://www.washingtonpost.com/news/local/wp/2016/12/04/d-c-police-respond-to-report-of-a-man-with-a-gun-at-comet-ping-pong-restaurant/?utm_term=.e5677882ef82

23 http://www.nytimes.com/2004/10/17/magazine/faith-certainty-and-the-presidency-of-george-w-bush.html

24 https://www.theguardian.com/us-news/2017/jan/11/trump-attacks-cnn-buzzfeed-at-press-conference

25 http://www.vox.com/policy-and-politics/2017/2/16/14640364/trump-press-conference-fake-news

26 Ed. Richard A. Posner, *The Essential Holmes: Selections from the Letters, Speeches, Judicial Opinions, and Other Writings of Oliver Wendell Holmes, Jr*, p. 320.

27 http://www.economist.com/newsbriefing/21706498-dishonesty-politics-nothing-new-manner-which-some-politicians-now-lie-and

3. CONSPIRACY AND DENIAL

1 http://harpers.org/archive/1964/11/the-paranoid-style-in-american-politics/1/

2 https://www.youtube.com/watch?v=zWlwZSM9z1E&feature=youtu.be

3 https://www.splcenter.org/fighting-hate/extremist-files/individual/alex-jones

4 http://publicmind.fdu.edu/2013/outthere/

5 https://www.washingtonpost.com/news/monkey-cage/wp/2015/02/19/fifty-percent-of-americans-believe-in-some-conspiracy-theory-heres-why/?utm_term=.104bf83fa030

6 http://prorev.com/center.htm

7   David Aaronovitch, *Voodoo Histories: The Role of Conspiracy Theory in Modern History* (2009).

8   Brotherton, op. cit., p. 242.

9   https://www.dartmouth.edu/~nyhan/nyhan-reifler.pdf

10 See Sara E. Gorman and Jack M. Gorman, *Denying to the Grave: Why We Ignore the Facts That Will Save Us* (2016); Specter, op. cit.

11 Brotherton, op. cit., p. 239.

12 See Gorman and Gorman, op. cit.; Specter, op. cit.

13 Specter, op. cit., p. 63.

14 https://www.nytimes.com/2017/02/23/opinion/the-anti-vaccine-movement-gains-a-friend-in-the-white-house.html

15 https://www.nytimes.com/2016/04/02/nyregion/anti-vaccine-film-pulled-from-tribeca-film-festival-draws-crowd-at-showing.html

16 For a comprehensive debunking of the 'CDC whistleblower' allegations see: http://scienceblogs.com/insolence/2016/03/22/wtf-andrew-wakefields-antivaccine-documentary-to-be-screened-at-the-tribeca-film-festival/; http://scienceblogs.com/insolence/2015/06/18/cranks-of-a-feather-the-nation-of-islam-teams-with-antivaccine-activists-to-oppose-sb-277/; http://scienceblogs.com/insolence/2016/01/05/the-cdc-whistleblower-documents-a-whole-lot-of-nothing-and-no-conspiracy-to-hide-an-mmr-autism-link/; and http://www.harpocratesspeaks.com/2014/09/mmr-cdc-and-brian-hooker-media-guide.html

17 Specter, op. cit., pp. 17–18.

18 Brotherton, op. cit., p. 36.

19 Brotherton, op. cit., p. 41.

20 Deborah Lipstadt, *Denying the Holocaust: The Growing Assault on Truth and Memory* (2016), p. 204.

21 Deborah Lipstadt, *Denial: Holocaust History on Trial* (2016), pp. 269–70.

22 Ibid., pp. 271–4.

23 https://www.theatlantic.com/international/archive/2014/05/
   the-world-is-full-of-holocaust-deniers/370870/

24 https://www.hks.harvard.edu/ocpa/pdf/HolocaustDenial
   PAE.pdf

25 Martin Ford, *The Rise of the Robots: Technology and the Threat
   of Mass Unemployment* (2016).

26 See Yuval Noah Harari, *Homo Deus: A Brief History of
   Tomorrow* (2016 English translation), *passim.*

27 http://nypost.com/2017/02/05/inside-amazons-robot-run-
   supermarket-that-needs-just-3-human-workers/

28 Brotherton, op. cit., p. 121.

29 John Irving, *The Cider House Rules* (1985)

4. THE CRASH OF THE PHILOSOPHER'S STONE

1 See, for an early and influential expression of this idea,
   Christopher Lasch, *The Revolt of the Elites and the Betrayal of
   Democracy* (1995).

2 http://spot.colorado.edu/~pasnau/seminar/berlin.pdf

3 Quoted in Simon Blackburn, *Truth: A Guide for the Perplexed*
   (2005), p. 76.

4 Quoted in ibid., p. 86.

5 Jean-François Lyotard, *The Postmodern Condition: A Report on
   Knowledge* (English translation, 1984), pp. xxiii–xxv.

6 Jean-François Lyotard, *The Inhuman: Reflections on Time*
   (English translation, paperback edition, 1998), p. 34.

7 Ibid., p. 116.

8 Ibid., pp. 203–4.

9 Jean Baudrillard, *Simulacra and Simulation* (English
   translation, 1994 edition), pp. 79–80.

10 See http://www.huffingtonpost.co.uk/andrew-jones/want-
   to-better-understand_b_13079632.html and https://www.

nytimes.com/2016/08/24/opinion/campaign-stops/the-age-of-post-truth-politics.html?_r=0

11 For a conservative critique of post-modernism, see Roger Scruton, *Fools, Frauds and Firebrands: Thinkers of the New Left* (2015), pp. 237–8.

12 http://www.politifact.com/truth-o-meter/statements/2015/nov/22/donald-trump/fact-checking-trumps-claim-thousands-new-jersey-ch/

13 https://www.theguardian.com/us-news/2015/nov/29/donald-trump-muslims-cheering-911-attacks

14 http://www.philosophynews.com/post/2015/01/29/What-is-Truth.aspx

15 Quoted in Jennifer L. Hochschild and Katherine Levine Einstein, *Do Facts Matter? Information and Misinformation in American Politics* (2015), p. 4.

16 https://www.unc.edu/courses/2009spring/plcy/240/001/Kant.pdf

17 Mary Poovey, *A History of the Modern Fact: Problems of Knowledge in the Sciences of Wealth and Society* (1998), p. xvi.

18 http://www.independent.co.uk/arts-entertainment/books/news/george-orwell-1984-alternative-facts-donald-trump-adviser-kellyanne-conway-amazon-sellout-bestseller-a7548666.html

19 George Orwell, *Nineteen Eighty-Four* (1978 paperback edition), pp. 171, 200–202, 212–13.

20 David Foster Wallace, *A Supposedly Fun Thing I'll Never Do Again* (1998 paperback edition), p. 67.

21 http://figureground.org/interview-with-maurizio-ferraris/

22 Maurizio Ferraris, *Positive Realism* (2015 edition), p. 33.

23 http://www.wcp2013.gr/files/items/6/649/eco_wcp.pdf?rnd=1375884459; Umberto Eco, *Kant and the Platypus: Essays on Language and Cognition* (English translation, 1999).

24 Blackburn, op. cit., p. 221.
25 Quoted in Blackburn, op. cit., p. 209.

5. 'THE STENCH OF LIES'

1   For the impact of the new technology, see, for instance, Adam Alter, *Irresistible: Why We Can't Stop Checking, Scrolling, Clicking and Watching* (2017).

2   https://www.bellingcat.com

3   https://www.nytimes.com/2017/02/06/business/syria-refugee-anas-modamani-germany-facebook.html

4   http://webfoundation.org/2017/03/web-turns-28-letter/

5   https://www.theguardian.com/media/2017/jan/12/bbc-sets-up-team-to-debunk-fake-news

6   http://www.pressgazette.co.uk/facebook-seeks-stronger-ties-with-news-industry-as-it-launches-journalism-project/

7   http://www.usatoday.com/story/tech/talkingtech/2017/01/24/snapchat-clamps-down-clickbait/96995456/

8   http://www.telegraph.co.uk/technology/2017/02/10/fake-news-killing-peoples-minds-says-apple-boss-tim-cook/

9   http://www.spectator.co.uk/2008/02/charlie-does-surf-meet-the-new-wizard-of-the-web/

10 Some continue to believe that peer-to-peer (P2P) action or 'peerist synergism' can defeat Post-Truth. See, for example, Layne Hartsell, *Post-Truth: Matters of Fact and Matters of Concern – The Internet of Thinking Together* (2017).

11 https://www.theguardian.com/politics/2017/feb/26/robert-mercer-breitbart-war-on-media-steve-bannon-donald-trump-nigel-farage

12 https://www.theatlantic.com/technology/archive/2016/12/how-computers-will-help-fact-check-the-internet/509870/

13 http://www.livescience.com/33512-pass-lie-detector-polygraph.html

14 Daniel Levitin, *A Field Guide to Lies and Statistics: A Neuroscientist on How to Make Sense of a Complex World* (UK edition, 2017), pp. 253, 216–21.

15 Viktor Mayer-Schönberger and Kenneth Cukier, *Big Data: The Essential Guide to Work, Life and Learning in the Age of Insight* (2017 paperback edition), pp. 164–6.

16 Gorman and Gorman, op. cit.

17 http://www.dailymail.co.uk/health/article-57944/Doctors-want-patient-time-doubled.html

18 See http://gking.harvard.edu/50c and http://jonathanstray.com/networked-propaganda-and-counter-propaganda

19 Alex Evans, *The Myth Gap: What Happens When Evidence and Arguments Aren't Enough?* (2017), p. xx.

20 Ibid., p. 14.

21 See Jonah Sachs, *Winning the Story Wars: Why Those Who Tell – and Live – the Best Stories Will Rule the Future* (2012). Also Brian Boyd, *On the Origin of Stories: Evolution, Cognition and Fiction* (2009).

22 Sachs, op. cit., p. 113.

23 https://www.theatlantic.com/daily-dish/archive/2008/09/identity-politics-from-milk-to-palin/211892/

24 http://www.vaclavhavel.cz/showtrans.php?cat=eseje&val=2_aj_eseje.html&typ=HTML

25 See Václav Havel, *Disturbing the Peace: A Conversation with Karel Hvizdala*, English translation by Paul Wilson (1990), Chapter 5.

26 http://www.telegraph.co.uk/news/politics/9434096/London-2012-Olympics-Boris-limbers-up-to-join-the-Tory-Olympians.html

27 http://www.thctimes.co.uk/article/we-all-made-a-terrible-mistake-on-migration-hr7qknsx8

28 http://www.independent.co.uk/voices/populism-facts-liberalism-social-media-filter-bubble-a7637641.html

29 Lipstadt, *Denial*, op. cit., p. 301.

30 See Hochschild and Einstein, op. cit., pp. 157–8.

31 http://washingtonmonthly.com/2009/04/10/poseys-delicate-sensibilities/

32 http://www.avclub.com/article/stephen-colbert-13970

33 http://www.telegraph.co.uk/news/2016/10/05/theresa-may-patriotic-speech-conservative-party-conference-live/

34 Quoted in Hochschild and Einstein, op. cit., p. 164.

35 http://www.parliament.uk/business/committees/committees-a-z/commons-select/culture-media-and-sport-committee/news-parliament-2015/fake-news-launch-16-17/

36 See Thaler and Sunstein, op. cit.; and Robert Cialdini, *Influence: The Psychology of Persuasion* (1984).

37 Hochschild and Einstein, op. cit., pp. 156–7.

38 'education alone is insufficient given inertia and incentives to remain with one's group in actively using misinformation' – Hochschild and Einstein, op. cit., p. 150.

39 Quoted in Hochschild and Einstein, op. cit., p. 166.

40 John le Carré, *The Secret Pilgrim* (1991 paperback), p. 336.

41 Winston Churchill, *My Early Life* (1930, 2013 ebook edition).

42 http://www.americanrhetoric.com/speeches/mlktempleisrael hollywood.htm

43 For a brilliant account of Kennedy's inaugural address, see Thurston Clarke, *Ask Not: The Inauguration of John F. Kennedy and the Speech that Changed America* (2004).

44 See Walter Isaacson, *Benjamin Franklin: An American Life* (2003), p. 459.

ABOUT THE AUTHOR

Matthew d'Ancona is the award-winning political columnist for the *Guardian*, *London Evening Standard*, *International New York Times* and *GQ*. Previously he was Editor of the *Spectator*, steering the magazine to record circulation. He is a Trustee of the Science Museum Group and chair of the think tank Bright Blue. He is a Visiting Research Fellow at Queen Mary University of London, and was elected a Fellow of All Souls College, Oxford, in 1989. He lives in south London.